Ten Things
I Wish I'd Known—
Before I Went Out
into the Real World

Ten Things

I Wish I'd Known—

Before I Went Out into the Real World

Maria Shriver

WARNER BOOKS

A Time Warner Company

Warner Books, Inc., 1271 Avenue of the Americas,
New York, NY 10020

Visit our Web site at www.twbookmark.com

A Time Warner Company

Printed in the United States of America
First Warner Books Printing: April 2000
10 9 8 7 6 5 4 3 2 1

Library of Congress Cataloging-in-Publication Data

Shriver, Maria.
    Ten things I wish I'd known—before I went out into the real world / Maria Shriver.
        p.   cm.
    ISBN 0-446-52612-6
    1. Youth—Conduct of life.   2. Shriver, Maria.   I. Title: Ten things I wish I'd known—before I went out into the real world.   II. Title.
BJ1661.S47 2000
158—dc21
                                                                                99-045651

Dedication

To my four beloved children . . . Katherine, Christina, Patrick, and Christopher. I thank you for the love, the laughter, and the fun you've brought into my life. I never knew how unconditional and deep love could really be.

To my wonderfully unique husband, Arnold. I thank you for the most fascinating adventure a gal could ever sign on for. If I'd known what a workout it was going to be, I would have gotten in better shape way back when. I love you, and thank you for helping me be all that I can be.

To my four glorious brothers, Bobby, Timmy, Mark, and Anthony. I can't believe I'm actually thanking you for tackling me, teasing me, and generally getting me ready for the real world. I wish every girl had the benefit of your training.

And to my extraordinary parents, Eunice and Sargent Shriver. There hasn't been a day in my life when I haven't felt your love, when I haven't heard your voices urging me forward, building me up, counseling me, and guiding me in the right direction. It would not be possible to have been loved more than I have been loved by you both, and there are no greater heroes in my life than the two of you.

XXXOO
Maria

Contents

Acknowledgments

·I could not have done this book without the wisdom, brilliance, guidance, support, and love of my mentor and dear friend, Roberta Hollander. She spent countless hours helping me in every way imaginable. She jogged my memory, tightened and polished my work, helped me put it all in context, and pushed me forward when I doubted myself and my thoughts. She has been my guiding light since I met her, and I am grateful beyond words to her for always, always, always stopping and being there for me.

I am also indebted to my other pals, all of whom played an invaluable part in the final outcome of this book. To my dear friend Oprah Winfrey—the first one who suggested that my speech would make a great book; to Julia Paige for all her encouragement—telling me on a daily basis that indeed I had to write this book; to Nadine Schiff, Wanda McDaniel, Michael Rourke, and Sandy Gleysteen, all of who read this book in its roughest form and offered me encouragement and constructive criticism; to Teri Hess, who went through it with a fine-tooth comb; to Jan Miller, the most dedicated and fearless of agents, and to her assistant, Shannon Miser-Marvin, who works on my behalf behind the scenes; to my sisters-in-law Linda, Alina, and Jeanne; my niece and nephews Rosie, Timbo, and Teddy. Thank you all for taking the time to help me with the cover, the print—the look—you were all so supportive and helpful; to Rick Horgan, who pursued this book before it was a book and waited patiently for me while I hemmed and hawed about whether to write it—his patience was worth a gold medal; and finally to all my new friends at Warner Books: Jackie Meyer, Emi Battaglia, Eric Wechter, Ralph Fowler, Tom Whatley, Ann Schwartz, Martha Otis, and Chris Barba. I thank you for your support, your belief in me, and for all the money that you've promised to spend on this great little book of mine.

Introduction

✤

I never meant to write this book. It grew from a speech I never wanted to give. I created both out of guilt, and now I'm thrilled I did. Let me explain.

Two years ago, Holy Cross College in Worcester, Massachusetts, invited me to give their commencement address. I hate to give speeches—hate it because I fear it. No matter how many speeches I give, it never gets any easier. I stress out for months in advance. What should I write? Why would anyone want to hear what I have to say? What *do* I have to say anyway? And I imagine every kind of disaster happening. What if I tell a joke and no one laughs? What if a good stiff wind comes, makes my hair stand on end, and blows my speech away? And more to the point: What if I sound like a damn idiot? What if I throw up? (I know, I know. If I'm so scared, how can I stand fearlessly in front of a television camera and blabber live to millions? It's because I can't *see* any of them.)

These obsessive thoughts and fears fry in my brain for weeks before I actually have to give the speech. My nerves are stretched thin. I'm jumpy and cranky and scared. Everyone in my life asks, "If you hate it so much, why on earth did you agree to speak in the first place?"

Well, in this case, as usual, I didn't agree right off the bat. When Holy Cross called, I wanted to thank them very much and politely say no. But there was a little problem. You see, one of my four brothers went to Holy Cross. His wife went to Holy Cross. My mother and my father both received honorary degrees from Holy Cross. And if that weren't enough, so did my uncle when he was president of the United States.

The head of the college made all of those points in the letter he wrote me. He listed them in the manner of an experienced Catholic priest used to getting his way, playing my guilt like a piccolo. His letter was plan A. But there was also a plan B—asking members of my family to make sure I knew how deeply important it was for me to give this speech. My brother called to lean on me. Yikes. Then my mother weighed in. I hemmed, I hawed. And like any good coward, I stalled for months.

So, Holy Cross went to plan C. They wrote me a note saying, in effect, that since they hadn't heard from me, they were moving on. The administration was disappointed, the faculty was disappointed, and of course, the students would be terribly disappointed. But clearly I was unable to commit, so they had to find someone else for whom this would be a great honor. I called my mother, I called my brother. Everyone said it was okay if I was scared to do it—but, boy, were they disappointed too.

It worked. It all worked. As the various plans unfolded, the guilt grew inside me, the pressure building up—until my resolve cracked wide open. You're RIGHT, all of you! I've been a horrible, worthless, spineless human being for saying no! And before I knew it, I was begging Holy Cross to *please* let me give the commencement address.

As soon as they said yes, I was sick to my stomach and back to prespeech hyperstress mode. Maybe I could still get out of it. I could get NBC to send me to the war in Yugoslavia on the same day. I could say one of my kids got sick. Or: "Terribly sorry. Gotta go interview the Pope." Surely a Catholic college would give me a dispensation for *that* one.

Unfortunately, no scenario I imagined eased the guilt I knew I'd feel if I didn't show up. And to tell the truth, I was getting whiplash from going back and forth. So finally I stopped resisting and got into action. I'd learned through long years of confronting fear that the only way to deal with it was to bulldoze my way through it. I started thinking.

What could I tell these kids getting out of college and getting into life? I thought back to what I was like when I was twenty-one and graduating—how numerous my options seemed and how little I knew about what would really happen to me. I started to wonder if my life would have been different if only I'd known THIS when I got out of college, or if only I'd known THAT. Pretty soon I had a list of THIS's and THATs and a theme for a speech. Well, look at me! Maybe I *did* have something that might interest these kids enough to get them to stop passing the beer and champagne and pay attention. What I had in my notes was all the stuff I wish *I'd* learned before stepping out into the Real World. I wrote and wrote and wrote, and it was actually fun. And I knew it was good when I read it out loud at the beauty parlor and everybody cried at the end and asked for a copy.

I was proud to give the commencement address at Holy Cross. I was proud they'd asked me and I accepted, proud I'd actually come up with a speech that seemed to move people. Most of all, I was proud I didn't throw up.

In fact, when it was over I got a standing ovation. Standing O's are common for commencement addresses, of course. Everyone is usually so relieved the speaker is finished, they just automatically jump up and cheer. But what happened after that *really* surprised me. Not only did students approach me to ask for copies. Parents came up with tears in their eyes saying how much they wished *they'd* known those same things when they were getting out of school. After the speech aired on C-Span and several other news shows, I was inundated with requests for it. Everywhere I went, men and women stopped me on the street to talk about it, to quote a line or two that had had an impact on them. No kidding. (That shocked me. People usually stop me on the street to ask about my husband's biceps or to offer up their own imitations of "I'll be back" with an Austrian accent.)

So in response to all the requests I received for this speech I never wanted to give, here is the book I never expected to write. All the points I made are the same. I've just expanded them. Putting something between covers wasn't a piece of cake either. When I was offered money to develop my commencement address into a book—*that's* when I went home and threw up.

So sit back and join me on a beautiful summer day in Massachusetts. The commencement address began like this:

> *Faculty, parents, family and friends, and graduates. I can honestly say I haven't been this excited since I learned how to spell Schwarzenegger.* [This got a big laugh.]
>
> *A couple of months ago Father Reedy phoned me and said, "Maria, do you believe in free speech?" I said, "Well, yes, Father, I do."*
>
> *"Well, that's terrific," he said, "because you'll be giving one in May at Holy Cross."*
>
> *Pretty clever, I thought. I called my brother and his brilliant friends who graduated from Holy Cross. "Give me the lowdown on this Father."*
>
> *They said, "Oh, he's a great guy. He's creative, he's funny,*

he's smart. He's an unbelievable fund-raiser." When I finally met him today, I didn't know whether to shake his hand or kiss his ring.

Father Reedy, I want to thank you for inviting me here. I'm deeply honored. Before I get going, I'd just like to take a moment to acknowledge all the parents here today. I know you're filled with great pride and, I'm sure, a great deal of relief as well, because you won't be seeing those big tuition bills anymore. As a parent of young children myself, I have some idea of what goes into getting your children to this place—lots of love, patience, understanding, and incredibly hard work. So I want to take my hat off to all the parents. I congratulate you.

On a personal note, I want to acknowledge my own parents, who flew here in the middle of the night from a Special Olympics board meeting in Europe. Mommy and Daddy, nothing makes me prouder than standing here in front of you to receive an honorary degree from a Catholic college and to give the commencement address. I love you.

I am honored to be here today on the twenty-fifth anniversary of the smartest policy decision Holy Cross ever made. I'm talking about the brilliant move a quarter century ago to upgrade the caliber and quality of the college by admitting women. [This got a huge round of cheers.] Women make a huge difference wherever they go. Believe me, I know what

I'm talking about. I'm the only girl in a family with four brothers, and I know how much I've enhanced and improved the quality of their lives—no matter what they say. And I, too, was educated at a formerly all-male Jesuit institution, Georgetown University.

As a matter of fact, gentlemen, let me torture you a moment. Close your eyes and just try to imagine Holy Cross without women. Horrible, right? Borrrrring! For that matter, try to imagine your life without women, period. Bet you can't. With no women around, you wouldn't know what to do with yourselves. And worst of all, you wouldn't even know that you didn't know—because there'd be no one here to tell you!

Because let's face it. We women may occasionally whine and pretend we're filled with self-doubt and fear and performance anxiety. But really, we know what we bring to the table: wit and intelligence and talent and creativity and superior intuition. Not to mention beauty, style, flair, taste—and forgive me, Mommy—Awesome Creative Sex. [This got a standing ovation from the entire student body.] *All in all, Holy Cross, you did good when you let women in.*

But I'm not here to talk about women. My goal today is to give each of you something you can take away with you. One word of wisdom. One idea that might help you in your life after Holy Cross. I've struggled to figure out what that message could be. Several students wrote to me suggesting my speech address their goals and their fears for what life will be like in the next century. Father Reedy suggested I tell you how I juggle career, motherhood, and marriage. I got an anxiety attack just thinking about that one. My mother and father suggested I talk about community service. My brother, Mark, the Holy Cross graduate, suggested I talk simply about him.

After much agonizing, I decided to share with you my top ten list of things I wish someone had told me when I was like you, sitting at my graduation, wondering when the commencement address was going to be over already. So here we go: Ten Things I Wish Someone Had Told Me at Graduation—Before I Went Out into the World.

That was the speech. Here comes the book . . .

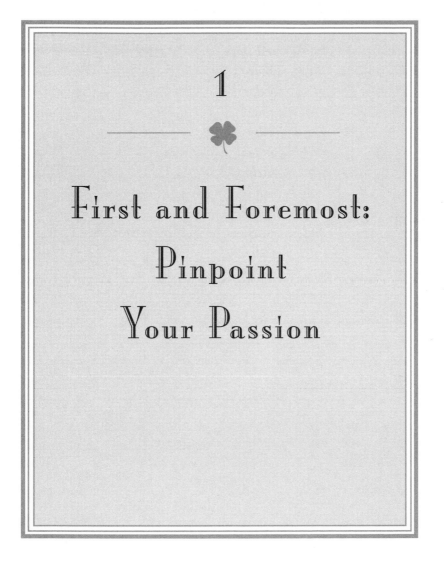

1

First and Foremost: Pinpoint Your Passion

B E HONEST WITH YOURSELF ABOUT IT. REALLY THINK about what you're interested in. What you enjoy, what captures your imagination and gets your brain going. What YOU want to do—not what you believe your parents or your teachers or society or your four brothers think you should do.

When I graduated back in 1977, all I wanted to do was anchor a network TV show. Everyone thought I was nuts. My parents' friends told me to get a grip on myself and go to law school until I could figure out what I really wanted to do. Others suggested I should catch the wave that was surely going to wash up on Wall Street. My girlfriends all wanted to go to the big city, get an apartment together, and have a blast. Still other people told me to get out of denial, stop fighting the family tradition, and go into politics. All legitimate goals, but they weren't mine.

I wanted to make a difference in people's lives, but not through the law or business or politics or public service. I wanted to tell the stories of the day in the medium of the day, television—reaching out to the world with ideas, made real in words and pictures.

Now, how had I gotten so passionate about going into television news? I was bitten by the bug back in 1972, when I was still in high school. As the ancient history majors among you may know, that year my father was the Democratic nominee for vice president. I was helping out on his campaign, and I was lucky to get the rare opportunity to travel on the campaign plane. (Note: If you have the inclination or the opportunity to work on an election campaign, grab it. I guarantee you'll learn more about people and politics in this country than almost anywhere else your travels may take you.)

My father's staff stuck me—"candidate's kid, obviously a brat!"—with "THEM" in the back of the plane. It turned out to be the best thing that ever happened to me. You see, the back of the plane was where the fun was, because "THEM" was the press, the hardworking, wisecracking guys (and a few women) from the big national media—newspapers, wire services, radio, and TV. Most of them had covered politics for years, watching the passing parade of candidates and campaigns through practiced (some would say jaundiced) eyes. They were constantly observing and commenting, and their endless stream of quips and coverage—even cartoons—put the presidential campaign on a whole new plane for me. Literally.

Remember, I'd lived and breathed politics my entire life—had political discussion and debate served like mashed potatoes with dinner every night since I was a little kid. In a lot of ways, politics and making history was the family business. But that year on the campaign, I experienced firsthand something groundshaking to me: I saw how the newspeople put their fingerprints on history before it *became* history, taking something that had just happened in front of my eyes and giving it context. What the public saw was not the raw event I was experiencing on the campaign. It was filtered and explained and shaped by the journalists first.

And as we traveled the country, this colorful, wonderful band of smart and funny explainers and shapers was constantly changing. Reporters and crews from local media would jump on board for a while and then drop off—people with regional interests, like agriculture in Wichita or unionism in Detroit, who'd put their own spin on it. And I also got to fraternize with and observe some of the real heavy hitters of political journalism. They'd travel with the campaign for varying lengths of time, and I'd eagerly await their pieces in the *New York Times* or the *Washington Post* or the *CBS Evening News* and scarf them up.

But the difference between regional and national reporters wasn't the only one I noticed. The straight reporters would report what they'd seen and heard—picking and choosing their story elements from what actually happened, but then just showing and describing them and letting readers or viewers come to their own conclusions. In contrast, the name columnists and commentators would get to interpret and analyze, offering their personal takes on what was going on in Campaign '72.

Either way, though, I saw it was the newspeople, not my dad or his press people, who decided what part of a speech, if anything, made it into the papers or on the air. By punching up certain issues or making the candidates the issue or focusing on the horse race, these journalists wielded huge influence. And it seemed to me that television had the most heat. It possessed an immediacy, an ability to capture and transmit the excitement (or the boredom) of the campaign—and the sincerity (or cynicism) of the candidates.

And it dawned on me right there in the back of the plane eating peanuts, that television would be the politics of the future. Television would be the way to touch people, move and excite them, anger and educate them the way politicians used to when they had direct contact with voters one-on-one in the streets. I knew this in my gut, and I wanted in.

Remember, this was the 1972 election, just a heartbeat before the Watergate scandal broke open. Before Bob Woodward and Carl Bernstein (let alone Robert Redford and Dustin Hoffman) intoxicated a generation with the ideal of crusading journalists exposing the bad guys to the light of the truth. In 1972, the news biz was not an obvious career choice, especially for a young woman.

So I sat in the back of the plane eating too many peanuts (more on that later), thinking, "Yes, this is for me." I, too, would travel the country and even the world, meeting people from every place and every walk of life. I'd hear their stories and then turn around and bear witness, sharing them with the rest of the country. I would be part of this pack of intense and highly competitive professionals. Work would never be boring. Laughter was a big part of it. And hadn't I always said I didn't want a desk job? These guys on the plane didn't even *have* desks.

Day after day, I asked my traveling companions every question I could think of. Where'd you go to school? What did you study? How did you get all of your experience? How do you handle the competition? What about that punishing deadline every day? Do you dread it or crave it? How many newspapers a day do you read? Five? How do you get scoops? How can you be so breezy, schmoozing politics with the other reporters, when your real goal is to beat the pants off them every night? When do you see your kids? I soaked up the answers, and my own dreams came into focus. By the time Campaign '72 was over, I knew what I wanted to do with my life—but I didn't tell a soul.

I didn't tell anyone because I thought they'd view it as silly, and I didn't want the hassle of trying to convince them otherwise. *I* knew otherwise, and that was enough. Also, part of it had just a little something to do with my family, which regarded the press in many ways as an adversary across a great divide—prying into our lives, chronicling our every move. Like many young people who are secretive about their dreams, I thought my family would be incredibly disappointed in my choice.

But remember, just because you *think* you must fulfill others' expectations doesn't mean you *have* to. And here's something shocking: You actually might be wrong. I was. When I finally told my parents what I wanted to do, they never once warned me not to. They never once told me I couldn't or shouldn't or wouldn't possibly succeed in the news business. They just nodded and said they regretted they couldn't really help me in that business, and they gave me their blessing. They might have thought I was silly or nuts, but they never let me know. They let me grow, and any skepticism they possessed changed into pride. Eventually.

Of course, my father's ticket lost the election in 1972. But not me. I won—a vision I could follow into my future, a passion I could pursue. It colored every decision I made after that— where I lived, where I worked, and who I spent time with. I was determined to learn everything I could about TV news, and I was determined to be good at it.

Lesson

Trust your gut, no matter what you expect your parents or teachers or anyone else will think of your choice. Lots of people don't know where to start. So try to pinpoint the field, the area, the kinds of people you want to be with. It's your life. Go with your gut.

2

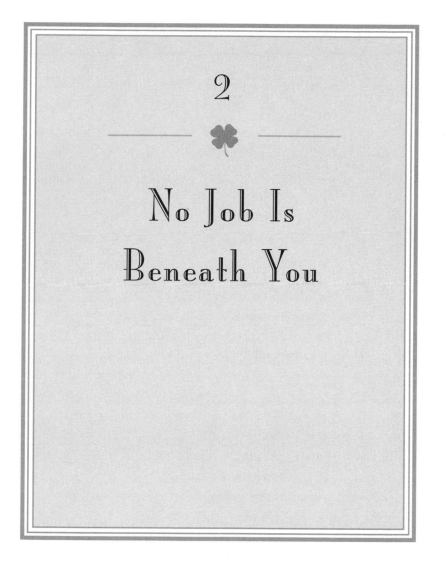

No Job Is
Beneath You

P ARENTS, FRIENDS, AND ACQUAINTANCES MAY REG-
ularly tell you you're smarter than Bill Gates and can do
anything you want. But I don't know anyone who hasn't
benefited from a willingness to start at the bottom. Even Bill
Gates began by doing odd jobs as a programmer.

Starting at the bottom builds character. It makes you hungry
and determined. It's also a very good way to find out, stunning as
it may be, that you're not as smart as you think you are. And it's
the best way to LEARN. Because if you haven't figured it out already, let me clue you in: There's a lot more to learn out there.
And you can learn it only by admitting you don't know it already,
which means starting at the bottom. Which is where I started.
Many times.

At the end of college, I focused on making my dream a reality. I applied to the Westinghouse broadcast training program—
sort of a glorified internship program for the TV stations the
company owned around the country. I was accepted into the

program, and right out of school headed off to KYW-T V in Philadelphia for my first job in television. Starting salary in the glamorous world of TV news: $12,000. I arrived in the newsroom bright-eyed, bushy-tailed, with a spanking new degree in American studies, and naive. Very naive.

I introduced myself to the news director, the guy who ran the station's news operation. In many ways, I have yet to recover. He was a local news veteran. He was tough, smart, opinionated, and determined to let me know immediately that HIS newsroom was NOT a place for rich little dilettantes like ME to amuse themselves until they got married. He wasn't quite sure how many strings I pulled to get this job that fifty deserving kids were DYING to get, but I was taking up space, and don't think he was happy about it. He explained to me that he didn't want and couldn't afford anyone in this newsroom who wasn't serious, who wasn't willing to work twenty-four hours a day, seven days a week, holidays included, night shifts, morning shifts—and how about a DOUBLE shift? He didn't need some twenty-one-year-old graduate from a fancy college—a RICH kid at that—coming in there thinking, "Ooooh, fun! Can I play with the cameras, too? Hey, I wanna go on the air!"

He spoke to me like no one ever had spoken to me. He said things no one ever had said to me. And he didn't care, because he was quite sure I wouldn't last and would be gone from there before anyone even noticed I'd arrived—because I was a

STRANGER, an INTERLOPER, and didn't belong in the hard-driving, hard-hitting, hard-boiled world of TV news, like HE did. And don't you forget it, you spoiled brat.

Wham-bam—hello? I walked out of his office, down the hall to the bathroom, locked myself in a stall, and cried my eyes out. That was the first and last time I ever cried at work. (Not the last time I ever cried *about* work. Just the last time I cried *at* work.)

I realized later the news director had the guts to say aloud to my cheerful little face what a lot of people were thinking: "Work? She doesn't have to work! Exactly what the hell is she doing here?" His words have stayed with me for more than two decades now, and I've remained in television news, weathering all the ups and downs, in part to quiet that critical voice echoing in my head. Sound nuts?

Well, I'm sure that news director wanted to break me. But instead, he helped make me. Because after I blew my nose and came out of the bathroom—and, I must admit, called my parents to tell them what the nasty man had said to me—I set out to prove him wrong.

There was nothing I wouldn't do in that newsroom. I worked my ass off. Dawn patrol, graveyard shift. Double shift? Yes, please. I worked weekdays, holidays, weekends, days and days on end. I worked wherever I could in the newsroom, because I didn't have my own desk. I scoured the wire services for stories for other people to do. I worked the assignment desk at 4 A.M.

Listened to police scanners for hours to get tips and leads. Worked the phones checking out stories and setting up shoots. I logged the real reporters' videotapes so they wouldn't have to. I answered the phones on the first ring. And I made that news director's damn coffee! And even smiled about it. This was *my* journalism school, and I constructed my own curriculum by finding out what no one else wanted to do and doing it.

You see, what the news director didn't recognize was that TV news was my *passion*. I wasn't at KYW to play around or get married or become famous. I was there for one reason only: to begin pursuing that passion. And this guy was indirectly fueling it by challenging it. He made me ask myself that very first day whether I could take the heat. Could I keep my eye on the prize way down the road? Did I have a fire in my belly? Because you need that conviction if you're going to be able to brush off criticism and negativity dished out by guys like that. And I knew he wouldn't be the last. So he bruised my ego, so what? I'll *use* him. I'll *learn* from him. I'll *show* him. And I did.

You know, maybe he was right. Maybe I was a brat. When what I want is out of reach, I keep climbing until I get it. I've had that kind of determination since I was a kid. And when you work that hard to pull yourself up, it really means something when you get there.

I stayed at the Philadelphia station until I completed the training program. (And by the way, when I was a reporter years later on a now defunct network newsmagazine in New York, I saw that Philadelphia news director again. He was a producer on the same show. I was terrified to see him. We said hello, that's all, and I never saw him again.)

After Philadelphia, I applied for and got a beginning field producer's job at WJZ, the Westinghouse station in Baltimore. I packed up my bags and drove south, still bright-eyed and bushy-tailed, but this time just a little less naive. Now, one of the advantages of starting at the bottom in the news biz is getting to work at these local stations—nonunion shops where everybody is allowed to do every job, so you can learn each aspect of the business hands-on. I was hired as associate-producer-slash-sound-technician. I was so thrilled to be moving up that I'd told WJZ *of course* I'd be able to run sound on a camera crew, in addition to my field-producing chores. Honestly, I had no concept of how to be a sound tech, so I was stretching the truth. But how hard could it possibly be?

Very. My Baltimore Experience started off insane. I remember nothing of the first few months, except working around the clock, around and around, all a big blur and whir in my memory. Sort of like a blackout. Or maybe it's one of those repressed memories—too painful to remember. I might be exaggerating this, but I think not. (I worked so much during my time in Baltimore, I never got the time to unpack the cartons in my apartment.)

As a soundwoman I was bad, dangerously bad. Sure, I'd always been able to work long hours, but I just didn't know how to do it with thirty pounds of sound gear on one shoulder. It felt like a ton. (Of course, now that I'm a four-time mother—no problem!) And not just get around. I had to run like a maniac to keep up with the cameraman I was attached to by a long audio cable. And believe me, I was no shrinking violet. I was what we call a big girl. And inept. There were so many cables and so many outlets and so many connectors and sockets and wires and plugs and microphones and windscreens—and I had absolutely no idea what went with what, and I couldn't seem to get it. I could not keep the gear straight. I was always trailing wires. The absolute rock bottom was the first time my reporter conducted an interview. When we got back to the station, there was no sound on the tape whatsoever. Not one belch, squeak, or pop. Nothing. And that was only the first time I came back with no audio.

No matter how hard I tried, I never got any better at all. But I'd never trade my time as The Worst Soundperson In History, because it was one of my best lessons in humility and acceptance of my own limitations.

Note: Everything does *not* come easy. Despite what Mom and Dad told you, you can*not* always do anything you set your mind to. I work with people who can do things I now know I just cannot do, and I accept it. Broadcast journalism requires a team effort to get on the air. I have the utmost respect for the editors, the camerapeople—and especially the sound technicians. Their work requires so much art and skill and knowledge, about audio, microphones, electronics, RF interference, and now digital everything—all things I'm constitutionally incapable of doing or learning.

I apologize profusely to all the camerapeople who put up with me as their sound tech in Baltimore. I know they joined me in being thrilled when the executive producer, in an act of self-preservation—actually it was a mercy killing—yanked me off sound duty.

So now I was free to concentrate on field producing—identifying stories, figuring out how to tell them, going out with the reporter and crew to gather all the elements, and coming back to write and put it all together in the edit room. I worked like a dog, and in the case of producing, I *did* get better and better at it. I stayed in Baltimore for two years and loved every second post-sound—the friends I made, the work I did, the opportunities I was given.

It was in Baltimore that I began to feel confident that if I could write and produce stories for others to read, I could also do it for myself. I hadn't wanted to go on the air until I felt I'd learned enough of the nuts and bolts behind the scenes to take care of myself in the field. I didn't want to be passive—just another pretty face who shows up to read words written by others, to narrate stories conceived by others. I wanted to be qualified to do it myself—conceive the story, report it, write it up, craft the piece, and deliver it with *my* name on it. I made a silent promise to myself: At my next job, I'd try to go on-camera. I didn't know if I was really ready, but I just had to give it a shot.

I left Baltimore to work in a political campaign—this one my uncle Teddy's run for the Democratic presidential nomination in 1980. When it was over (sooner than we would have liked, but that's another book), I went to a few TV agents to see about getting an on-camera job. The meetings were memorable, because not one of the agents was the least bit encouraging. Encouraging? How about this: One of the biggest agents in the business—still is—told me point-blank to forget it, he could *never* send me out for a job until I lost twenty-five pounds and did something about my nasal voice. Twenty-five pounds! (Remember, I told you we'd get back to those peanuts. I'd never stopped with the peanuts.)

I'll never forget that meeting as long as I live. I left the office with my head held high—and cried my eyes out in the car. I was so ashamed. I was so mortified. I was so angry at the agent for his casual cruelty. I called my parents, who were horrified: "Of *course* you're not fat! Your voice isn't shrill! We've never heard *any*body say that about your voice! You are not fat and shrill at all!" Naturally the people who love you try to build you up. But inside, I knew that once again a brutally honest person was telling me something I needed to hear. If you're going to pursue your passion to its fulfillment, sometimes you have to confront uncomfortable things about yourself and change them. I could either continue eating the way I was or turn it around. Once again, I had to just blow my nose and move on—trying to seize humility from the jaws of humiliation. "Okay, if that's what it takes, here we go."

I'd always struggled with my weight—up and down, up and down—but now I looked at weight loss as a full-time job, a campaign. I went on an intense, strict diet. I exercised like a maniac, wrote down everything I ate, the whole nine yards. I found a voice coach and went to her several times a week. I worked on myself like a woman possessed, keeping my eye on the goal. And several months later, I was back in the agent's office demanding that he help me, because I'd followed his advice. He tried, but the truth is, the jobs he was sending me on really required more on-air experience than I had, which was none. If I wanted to do it, I'd have to start at the bottom. Again.

Within a few months, I got a small break. A syndicated music show was starting, and they needed someone to go out in the field and interview legends in the music business—stars like Aretha Franklin and Alice Cooper. Even though I'd conduct the interviews, I wouldn't appear on the air. But I *was* able to get footage of myself on location to use for an audition reel. Television is like any other business. You grab whatever you can to move yourself forward.

Right about the same time, Westinghouse was in the process of syndicating their own highly successful local magazine show, *Evening Magazine,* into a national broadcast called *PM Magazine.* Fortunately, I had produced for their local show in Baltimore. Since I was already a member of the Westinghouse family, the producers took a look at my new on-air audition reel. They were willing to give me a shot on-camera. After all, they already knew I would hustle, that I'd come cheap, and that if it didn't pan out I could always go back to field producing for them. (Note: Be careful not to burn bridges when you leave a job. You never know when you'll have to ask the very same people to help you again.)

So at last I was on the air, and I was thrilled. For two years I was a national correspondent for *PM Magazine* working out of Los Angeles, and I had a blast. It wasn't *60 Minutes,* but what else *was* at that time? Few people ever get to *60 Minutes*—and hardly anyone starts off there. And so what if I wasn't covering war and politics and doing only light features? There was a lot of work, a lot of travel, a lot of opportunity. I was on the air and on my way. Having fun, and learning, learning, learning—growing more and more comfortable within my own skin in the TV business.

I always get a chuckle when young people come up to me and say, "I wanna do just what you're doing," and go on to explain that, of course, they realize it'll take them a few years. They fully expect they can be Tom Brokaw or Barbara Walters by the time they're thirty. Listen: You can't short-circuit the learning process. It takes time to get to the top, and that's good—because by the time you get there, you'll have learned what you need to know in order to stay there.

So relax, take your time, and don't be in such a rush. And remember: No job is beneath you. But also know that on your way up, you may run into critical and judgmental people, jealous people—people who may say you got where you are because of who you are or what you are, what school your father went to or what you look like or who you knew when. No matter. Shake it off. If they have a problem with you, it's their problem, not yours. Just shelve your ego, put your head down, and bulldog forward, grinding it out. There is no better way to gain respect—and self-respect—than through hard work.

Lesson

Starting at the bottom is not about humiliation. It's about humility—a realistic assessment of where you are in the learning curve. And be honest with yourself. Learn what you're not good at and appreciate those coworkers who are. Just stay away from the sound equipment. And the peanuts.

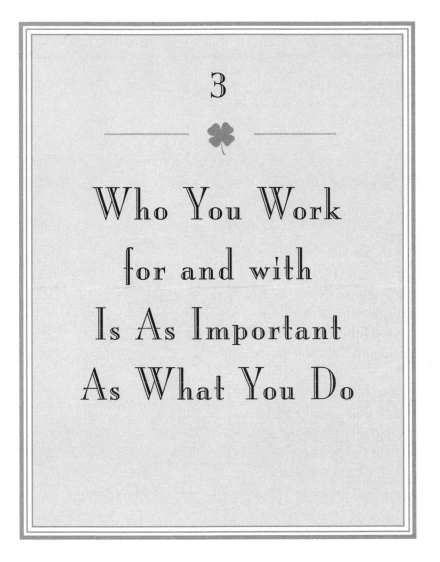

3

Who You Work for and with Is As Important As What You Do

I T'S TRUE. IT'S BETTER FOR YOUR CAREER AND FOR YOUR soul to be in a lowly job working for a great boss than being the head of—oh, let's just say the highly rated *Jerry Springer Show.* I've learned this through experience.

After busting my butt at the Philadelphia station and then busting my brains in Baltimore and Los Angeles, I got a huge break. I was hired by CBS News to be a junior reporter on the *CBS Morning News,* working out of the L.A. bureau. This was the network news that I was always aiming for! I was in! At the bottom again, but in! In over my head and terrified.

I need to tell you that I survived there—and even thrived there—not because I was so great, but because a brilliant, wise-cracking, hard-of-hearing, tough-nosed producer happened to be in a good mood the day I asked her for help. Now, she was a street-savvy veteran from Brooklyn and I was— well, let's just say, not from Brooklyn. We couldn't have been more different. I don't think anyone who knew either of us imagined we would ever get along, much less become friends.

When the powers that be in the CBS L.A. bureau told me they were assigning this incredible producer to work with me, I was mightily impressed. They told me she'd started with CBS back at the Radio Network, that she was a great writer and producer. She'd worked with Walter Cronkite and Hughes Rudd. Wow! She knew all the players and procedures. She was great on deadline and knew her way around microwave and satellite trucks. She would always get me on the air. Most important, she'd teach me all about writing and story structure.

I was crazy with excitement. CBS News likes me! They're interested in cultivating me, nurturing me, teaching me! They're going to invest time and talent in my career! When can I meet this great lady?

Oh, in just a few weeks, they said. That's when your producer is getting out of a drug rehabilitation program in the desert, and you two can get right down to work. Whoa.

What they didn't tell me about my producer was that she made the maniacal producer in *Broadcast News* look like a sleepwalker. Her life had spun so out of control personally and professionally that CBS had sent her away to clean up. Oh, boy. I told you I wouldn't be bored.

What I also didn't know until much later was what happened at about the same time out in the desert, when *she* found out she was going to work with *me*. She was in group therapy at the treatment center when the counselor read her a letter from CBS News informing her that when she came back to work she wasn't going to be a hard-news producer anymore. "We're hiring Maria Shriver, and you are going to help make her a star."

She leapt up and started screaming. "A Kennedy kid? They hired a Kennedy kid? They hate me so much that I have to work with a Kennedy kid? They're punishing me!" She was humiliated, devastated, enraged. To her, and I'm sure most other veterans, I represented everything that was going wrong with the news business. Not only did I come from a famous family, I hadn't gone to journalism school, I hadn't worked in the business for years before coming to the network, and worst of all I was young, not bad-looking, and dating an Austrian bodybuilder who thought he could be a movie star. No wonder my producer thought CBS had lost its mind and her career was over. Looking back, I'm sure the bosses at CBS News thought we'd either kill each other or quit. Two less problems for them.

I'll never forget the first time I met her. I was *sooo* thrilled. I waited for her to come out of the bureau manager's office her first day back from treatment. I stuck out my hand and said, "Hi, I'm Maria. I'm so excited to meet you." She looked at me, rolled her eyes, and kept walking. I followed her like a puppy dog. Perhaps she hadn't heard me. I reintroduced myself and babbled on about how great this was and what a killer team we'd make. She waited until I was finished and then looked me dead in the eye. She explained that she hadn't heard a word of what I'd said because she was hard of hearing and her hearing aids were off. She went on—and I'm paraphrasing, because most of it is unprintable—that she would be working with me only because she had to. That she considered it a demotion, but she supposed she had to pay dues for behaving like a maniac all those years. That her main priority in life was not making me a star but staying clean, learning how to live without drugs, and paying off her drug debts. Teaching me was at the bottom of the totem pole. All of a sudden my news director in Philadelphia looked like a pushover.

I remember our first few stories extremely well. My producer had no respect for me and didn't care if I knew it—and seemed to want everyone else to know it, too. Whenever we were out on a story, I'd make suggestions—"Why don't we shoot this?" or "Why don't we set up the interview over here?"—because after all, I *had* been producing for a few years. In response, she'd make a big show of turning off her hearing aids so she could "pretend" she hadn't heard—indicating *I* couldn't possibly have anything useful to offer.

When we got back to the bureau I'd write the script and hand it to her for editing. She'd read it and make a sour-lemon face and start motormouthing directions: "This script is s——. You buried the lead in the third paragraph. It goes up here. Always put the attribution at the beginning of the sentence. Don't lead into a sound bite by telling us exactly what the person is saying before they say it. And don't tell me I'm seeing an apple. This is television, and I can see the apple with my eyes. Tell me something else. Don't tell me the father is crying while you're showing him crying. Tell me what you learned about him because you were there." She crossed out sections of script with big slashes of her red pen, yelling, "This is bla-bla!" She drew arrows moving sentences around. She screamed so that everyone in the office could hear. Then she'd send me back to my cubicle for rewrite after rewrite after rewrite, until she could say, "Yes. There's no more bla-bla. This is tight. I can make this into a piece."

She screamed about my voice-overs: "You sound like a *Saturday Night Live* news satire!" She yelled at me when we got assigned to entertainment stories: "You're flushing my career down the toilet!" She chased me around the newsroom hollering, "Accuracy! If we don't have accuracy, we don't have s———!" She kicked me out of the editing room with "Leave me alone. I'm trying to make you look good!" And so she did. And I watched, and I learned.

We spent so much time together, I knew at some point she would have to really talk to me. So I just waited. I kept my ears open in the car, when she'd tell the crew she was still thinking about drugs all the time and couldn't sleep at night. And I realized that what she was doing—struggling day in and day out to stay clean—was a far bigger deal than what I was doing, learning TV news. I just kept my head down and watched her and kept going to her for help.

And pretty soon it changed. She barged into my office one day, slammed the door, and cried, "I can't do this anymore. I'm gonna go out and get loaded."

I yelled back, "Don't be ridiculous! Don't you know how much courage you have? Don't you know how much courage it takes to do what you're doing?"

"I don't have any courage. It's too much pressure. I'm not gonna make it."

"Well, you are gonna make it. Get your butt to one of those anonymous meetings you go to." And she did. I think right then we accepted that we both had something to prove to ourselves and the company we worked for—but that we didn't have to prove it to each other. Also that there was a lot we could learn from each other. From then on, each of us refused to allow the other to be overcome by her fears, and the trust grew.

We went on to become an incredible team. She still would slash at my scripts, screaming, "Bla-bla! Too much bla-bla!" But we would laugh about it—and so would everyone else in the bureau. And as we worked and laughed, I got better at doing news, and she got better at doing life. We traveled around the world reporting every kind of story: murders, political conventions, the

Olympics, the Cannes Film Festival. You name it, we did it on the spot.

Take boxing. When our boss assigned us the world middle-weight championship fight between Marvelous Marvin Hagler and Roberto Duran in Las Vegas, the conversation went like this.

"Do you know anything about boxing?"

"No. You?"

"Nope."

"Let's go!"

In Las Vegas, my producer made sure the editor assigned to us was our bureau boxing expert. Since we didn't have television rights to the fight, my producer had to bring a still photographer and arrange to have the film developed immediately so we could make the East Coast morning deadline with my fight commentary. Fight commentary? How could I possibly give fight commentary?

In most businesses, you learn on the job. But in the news business you have to learn really fast, even becoming an instant expert. You get thrown into a story in a flash and hit the ground running. You have to ask the right questions of the right people and listen and learn.

When I got to Caesar's Palace (and I went alone, because we had only one press pass), I figured the right people were the reporters who cover boxing for a living. I went to several who were sitting ringside, people like Dick Schapp of ABC News and the guys from *Sports Illustrated*. I asked them for technical help describing the fight: "Here's a piece of paper. Could you please jot down a few notes—who hit whom with a left jab or a right uppercut in what round? Whatever you can do will be appreciated. I'll come get the paper when it's over." They were amused. (You know, people who are really good at their game are generous with their gifts, not stingy with them.)

It was called "the fight of the year," and it certainly felt that way to me. Fifteen rounds of fury—and that was just what was going on in the edit room. We studied the notes with our editor and figured out the highlights—for instance, Hagler got Duran with a right jab in the first round, Duran hit Hagler with hard rights to the face in the twelfth. The editor matched up the pictures, we punched up the drama with my own observations, and we sewed together the fight. It was dramatic, and it was right on the money. By the way, that night our edit gear was set up in a bathroom at our Las Vegas station. I had to record my narration in between the toilets flushing. TV news is very glamorous.

In the end, Marvelous Marvin kept his title—and my marvelous producer and I got to do a couple more boxing pieces for our show.

All these years later, we're still the closest of friends, and I still say that pretty much everything I learned about television news, I learned from her. Put it this way: I was employed by

CBS News, but I really worked for her. She challenged me, she encouraged me, she guided me—and when I screwed up, she screamed at me, usually in four-letter words. She warned me about the temptations and the pitfalls and the ethical land mines. But she also stoked that fire burning within me: to dig for the story, to find the truth, and then to turn around and tell it to the public, accurately, artfully, ethically, and well. That is what she taught, and those are principles I try to adhere to today. There is no doubt in my mind that had I not possessed the humility to ask her over and over again for help—and had I not *listened* to her when she gave it to me—I would never have survived my first years in the network news business. Even now, when I have doubts and concerns—and I do—I call her for guidance. She remains one of my best friends, and I'm so proud that she's stayed clean to this day.

Lesson

God puts mentors in your path. They may not look like you, sound like you, or be what you expect. But they always know more than you, and that's the whole point. Use them. If you don't find one at the beginning of your career, that's okay. Keep your eyes open. Mentors will cross your path later on. They transmit the lessons you need to learn. Like this next one:

4

Your Behavior Has Consequences

O UCH! WELCOME TO ADULTHOOD. YOUR PARENTS, your friends, society, the business world—no one but you is responsible for how you conduct yourself. You are not a victim. The single most important determining factor in your life is you. And it's never too early to get your ethical act together.

Be strong about what you believe in. Be firm about who you really are—plus and minus. Know what you will and won't do to get ahead. Know what you can and cannot live with. Believe me, this is a big one. Your job will test your ethics—and therefore *teach* you ethics—every day.

Let's face it, life after college is different with a capital D. You're out in the real world full-time, and people expect you to act accordingly. But you're not a cork bobbing on the wild and wicked ocean, tossed and turned by powers beyond your control—even if it feels that way. Other people's ethics do not have to be yours. You and you alone are responsible for how you behave. Yes, you do have to learn the rules of engagement in your chosen field. But if you ignore what *you* know to be the difference between right and wrong, you'll pay a huge price. And I'm not just talking about losing sleep.

I think it's pretty safe to assume if you have a great job, someone else has an eye on it, too. What will you do to keep that awesome job? To what lengths will you go? I found myself asking those questions not all that long after I got to CBS News.

As I was getting better on the air, there was a well-known anchorwoman, who also happened to be a friend of mine. The network had hired her with great fanfare, as usual, but it turned out she wasn't bringing in the ratings. It was no surprise in the morning news business—a meat grinder that chews people up and spits them out—that the network wanted her out. God forbid they should tell her to her face. All of a sudden I found myself being assigned stories that should have been hers. I knew it was designed to make her feel insecure. They had me do on-camera intros live from her anchor desk, right next to her. Anything I could do to breathe down her neck and make her feel threatened. Keep in mind, these were grown-ups with big jobs who were hoping that this woman would just buckle under the pressure and leave on her own. And I was the obvious anchor-in-waiting ready to plunk right down in her chair. I've since learned that this kind of maneuvering is standard operating procedure for many network executives. They come up with "quick-fix" strategies and probably forget about them the next day.

But I was so new at the game, it all made a deep impression on me. I went to one of them and said, "You know, this isn't my style. I want the job, but not this way."

Now, I'm no Mother Theresa. I admit I did enjoy the increased air time and attention. And it would have been so easy to rationalize: These people had powerful network jobs because they were older and wiser than me, and that's just the way the business is. But that's just not true. I can't blame the boss or the business if my own footsteps cross an ethical line. If my gut tells me it's wrong, that's the signal *not to do it.* I can't *know* it's wrong and *do* it anyway, and then *blame* the corporate culture to get myself off the hook. *I'm* the one who's responsible for my actions.

Bottom line: I refused to squeeze out my friend. She moved on anyway, and I never had to be embarrassed when I looked her in the eye nor feel I'd done something evil to her. And those people who asked me to do those things? They don't have those great big jobs anymore.

Here's another story to illustrate my point. Years later, a producer sent me out to do a follow-up on a story we had worked on together. After a month setting it up, I made a final call to our story subjects to confirm our shooting arrangements. They revealed in an offhand way that the producer had bought the rights to their story, hoping to sell it as a TV movie. Whoa! I realized right there and then he was using me and the show to promote his own TV project. I knew it was wrong. In fact, we're not *allowed* to do news stories for personal profit—and the producer's own gut must have told him it was wrong, too, because he'd kept it a secret. I was hurt and confused. I also was furious, because if I put my name and face on the story, people would think I must have known about the business arrangement and therefore condoned it. I immediately took myself off the assignment. Consequence: A great story was killed, a working relationship was damaged, and the producer's reputation took a hit—and in the news business, as in many others, your reputation is everything.

We all develop our own ethical standards, figure out exactly where is that fine line we won't cross. And my gut tells me there's more at stake than just right and wrong. It's probably the Black Irish in me, but I also adhere to the superstition that what goes around comes around and bites you in the butt. So watch it.

As the competition in the news business stiffens, the pressure has grown unbelievably intense. There are more shows, more producers, more people like me competing for the same great "get" (the top interview subject of the day). There's an almost unbearable temptation to tear down someone else in order to further yourself. I'm talking about bad-mouthing the competition to get the subject to talk to me and not to her: "Oh, you don't want to do *her* show. It's not prestigious enough! My audience is much bigger! Anyway, she won't mind doing you after I do." Believe it or not, that's what sometimes goes on among the

high-pay, high-profile correspondents competing for the top interviews.

Now, I don't want to sound holier-than-thou. To be truthful,
I've engaged in these conversations: "If you don't do my show
first, forget it. I can't do it." That kind of manipulation has come
out of my mouth more times than I care to admit. In fact, it wasn't
until a well-known woman in my business told me she'd heard
what another well-known journalist had said about *her* that I
really started to watch my words when I make my pitch. Win-
ning by running down my competitors isn't the kind of person I
want to be.

How do you get your gut to talk ethics to you? You already
know how. The ethical and spiritual lessons you've learned from
your parents, your teachers, and your religion are internalized
down there and talk back to you, guiding you through life. The
problem is hearing it. When the pressure is intense, you have to
take the time to stop and have a conversation with yourself, re-
flecting on what your own ethics are, what you've been taught.

And the process never stops, which is why we need mentors.
They not only teach us how to do our work, they teach us the
specific ethical principles of our profession. When I first got to
CBS, they made me read and reread the *CBS News Standards
and Practices Manual.* And my crazy producer went one better:
She bludgeoned me with them, so I'd learn the wrongs and
rights of journalistic practice.

"Don't stage anything on a story. We just record what happens. We don't make it happen.

"Don't tell someone you're doing a story about one thing when it's really about something else.

"Don't let a story subject buy or give you anything.

"Don't . . . don't . . . don't." That was my foundation.

As you go along, make sure you identify people whose professional lives and ethical choices you admire. Then if you're asked to do something dicey or questionable and you get a slight gnawing in your gut—ASK! They'll give you the additional ethical and spiritual guideposts you need as you pursue your own success.

Sometimes your teachers pop up unsummoned. After I'd been at CBS for a while, I did some pieces for (yet another) now defunct magazine show. This day, we were at an Orange County, California, trailer park that had been there since the county really was mostly orange groves. But now developers were seizing the land and throwing the people out. At a nighttime residents' meeting, one of the organizers said, "We have a very special visitor with us—Maria Shriver of CBS News." People applauded and cheered, and I took that as a signal to go to the front of the room and make a little speech. I went into full-on rousing Democratic Party up-with-the-people campaign mode. I told them how glad I was to be able to get their side of the story out, that they were being mistreated by Big Business, and they were the Little People whose voice deserved to be heard. I got a standing ovation. Flush with victory, I returned to my crew in the back of the room.

Whereupon the cameraman—a veteran newsman, one of the original electronic cameramen in this country—yanked me outside. "Don't you *ever* do that again. You are a journalist, not a politician. You are not here to further anybody's cause. You are here to get the people's side of the story, then get the developers' side of the story, and then tell the story honestly and fairly and get out. That's it. They didn't applaud you because you're such a great reporter. They cheered because you're a celebrity. What you did was unprofessional. Don't do that again." I know if he didn't care about me, he could have videotaped that little disaster and gotten me fired. He didn't—and I learned one more lesson from one more loving teacher.

The life lessons my own parents gave me are probably the ones I've most relied on. If I'd known how much I'd need them in my profession, I would have listened even better. My father has always been highly respected, because he carries himself with intelligence, humor, dignity, and class. He's the one who taught me it's never worth stabbing someone in the back to get ahead. He said that talent and smarts always win out, that if you're good, you'll get the great job. He said never let a puffed-up ego make your decisions for you. That's a hard one if you're a driven person like me, because chances are you've got a sizable ego, too. He taught me to make sure to have people around me honest enough to tell me when my overreaching ego is about to get the better of me.

My mother is the one who taught me to be a bulldog, to forge my own way around and through problems and obstacles. Like my father, she's a stickler for honesty and responsibility. She told me—and taught me by example—that when I screwed up, I should admit it, take responsibility for it, not blame it on anyone else, and then move on.

My parents also instilled in me a strong work ethic. They taught me to respect people who show up day in and day out and do a full day's work for a full day's pay, to admire people who work at two and even three jobs to take care of their families. My mother always said, "You're lucky to have a job and lucky to do something you love."

My parents also infused in their children the necessity for community service—to give back some of what was given to us. My father started the Peace Corps, Job Corps, and Head Start, among other programs in the 1960s. My mother went against all known theories about what mentally disabled people could do and started the Special Olympics. All of my parents' programs give people an opportunity to volunteer, get involved, share the abundance. This is a family tradition that enriches our spirits, and my husband and I are trying to pass the gift along to our children—so they'll grow up world-centered instead of self-centered, with generous hearts like their grandparents.

My mother also drilled this message into me: "Don't depend on your looks." Every time people would tell me I was attractive, my mother would be right behind them warning me that the world was filled with attractive women, that looks came and went, and if I wanted to achieve anything in life, I'd have to do it with my brains. Now, my appearance has definitely helped me, no doubt about it. In the television business it always helps to look good. But I believe it's also a profession where you can survive and succeed only if you're tough, tenacious, smart, and careful about your reputation. You cannot survive if you cut corners, lie, or bend the truth.

Lesson

Situational ethics just don't cut it. The end (the dream job) does not justify the means (screwing a colleague). I know it sounds easy for me to say that we should all stand our ethical ground. After all, if someone fires me for opening my big mouth, I'll still have food on the table. Still, I believe all of us rise when we work with principles we believe in consistently—and when we work with people who believe and behave the same way.

When you cut corners with what you know is right, you're risking your good name, your reputation. It's bigger than the promotion, the money, or the deal. It's who you are. Don't give it away so fast.

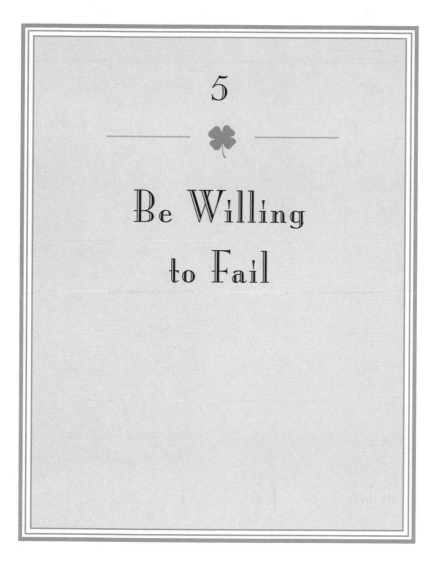

5

Be Willing
to Fail

I'M SORRY TO HAVE TO TELL YOU THIS, BUT MANY OF YOU will experience failure in the pursuit of your passion. Many of you will fail to attain some of the goals or fulfill some of the dreams you have right now. But it's incredibly important to understand that FAILING IS PART OF LEARNING. Fear of failure can paralyze you. If you don't risk looking ridiculous or inept or even stupid sometimes, you may stay secure, but you'll also stay the same. By avoiding failure, you're also avoiding life's richness. And what happens if you fail? It can be liberating. In fact, I've found most people who've achieved great success also have experienced some great defeat. I wish someone had told me *that* on graduation day. Instead, everyone told me I could go ahead and do anything I wanted, be anyone I wanted to become, with no detours or U-turns in my path. The hidden message was this: If you fail, shame on you. Well, that's not true.

Remember, my first big goal out of college was to anchor a network news show. Well, I realized that dream eight years later in 1985, when I became the coanchor of the *CBS Morning News*. I recall every minute of that job as clearly as when I lived it.

You can't imagine how thrilled I was to anchor that broadcast. Or how much it meant to get equal billing and equal compensation with my coanchor, Forrest Sawyer. In my mind I was on my way. Now that I had this job, nothing could or would stop me. I was finally a member of the elite club of women anchoring the national morning shows—and to me, that was heaven.

In fact, my head was so high up in the clouds that I was oblivious to the brutal behind-the-scenes maneuvering of network television executives back on earth. Now, I wasn't a *total* idiot. I knew that when Forrest and I took over the *CBS Morning News* it was in third place behind *Good Morning America* and the *Today* show. I knew we were rookies following in far bigger footsteps than ours—bigger names who'd never been able to push the show into first place. But I assumed we'd be given a fair shot and dealt with openly and honestly. Guess I was still naive.

I tried not to pay too much attention to the reviews. Well, that's a lie. How could I *not* pay attention, when I was reading this in the *Washington Post*:

Forrest Sawyer . . . is partnered on the program with Maria Shriver's hair. Shriver does not look as if she cares about the answers to many questions except "Where's my brush?" and "What time will Arnold be home?" She sucks in her cheeks and deflates her face, looking a little like one of those cartoon characters who got slipped a dose of alum.

All righteeee! It's going to be personal. Hair reviews. This is what we're up against. The scrutiny could be excruciating, but I tried to stay above it—sort of like staying above churning whitewater rapids on a little raft. I just figured when you got in this particular river, you were going for a ride.

And a ride it was. During the year I anchored the morning news, there were three different executive producers—two men and a woman all trying to prove themselves with three different agendas, three different concepts for fixing the show, and three different plans for making us anchors more appealing. In general, they thought Forrest was too stiff, and they wanted him to loosen up. As for me, they wanted a total overhaul. Starting, of course, with my hair, which had made it into the *Washington Post.*

"Your hair. Too long. Cut it. It's much too distracting."

"Your hair. Too dark. Lighten it. Blonde is better with breakfast."

"Your hair's too *there.* Your eyes, your voice—you're just too *much* in the morning."

"Don't laugh on the air. It's unprofessional."

"No more bright colors. You're too threatening to women."

As you might imagine, with so much of me in need of fixing, I felt just a touch insecure. But since the producers were the ones running focus groups and doing audience research, I figured they had to know what they were talking about. I tried to keep my attitude really positive. And somehow over the year, with all the management zigzagging, we still moved the ratings up to numbers they haven't seen since. I was proud of our work, and I was learning, evolving, and growing.

After we'd been in the hot seat almost a year, the networks sent all the morning news shows to London to cover the royal wedding of Prince Andrew and Sarah Ferguson. It was the summer of '86, and I remember it clearly—not just because we delivered hours and hours of terrific live television, not just because we had great guests, and not just because the shows were lively, edgy, and interesting. I remember it because of what happened afterwards.

The staff of our show congregated in the London bureau, congratulating each other and speculating on how long the royal marriage would last. What we didn't know was the marriage would last longer than we would.

The network president came into the London bureau, and in the time-honored tradition of network executives everywhere, he congratulated us on our work, told us how wonderful our team was, and left. Later that same day we got the word—by

fax!—that the *Morning News* had been canceled. Not just Forrest and me, but the whole damn show. Boom. Just like that, finished. As someone I know once said, "Hasta la vista, baby."

Note: People in your business will lie to you. Some even
will lie straight to your face—a tremendously shocking idea to
me back then. Call me naive—or better yet, call me an idiot—
because I should have seen the handwriting on the wall
months earlier, when this item appeared in the newspaper:

> Newlywed Maria Shriver, coanchor of the *CBS Morning
> News*, is expected to leave the job in several months "for
> personal reasons," according to top sources at the net-
> work. She's eager to shed the grueling grind at CBS and
> move back to the West Coast to be with her husband
> full-time. Insiders report that CBS News management
> did not try to argue her out of the move.

What? I was stunned. I'd never had any such conversation,
never said such a thing, never even thought it. Where'd they get
that story? Isn't that silly. I asked my bosses about it, and they
acted—and "acted" is the operative word here—shocked. They
couldn't imagine where the newspaper got the story either. Oh
well, I told myself, it must not be true, so don't pay any attention
to it. Yeah, right. I was too naive to know that the "leak" to the

paper was a shot across the bow from the bosses, one of whom was quoted shortly thereafter as saying,

> We are very optimistic about the *Morning News* with Maria Shriver and Forrest Sawyer, and I see no reason why we would make changes in that lineup.

"See?" I told myself. "They love us."

Well, months later, that was one of the guys who canned us. I was devastated, humiliated, and pissed off. I'd never really failed at anything. Oh sure, there were little setbacks—remember how I crashed and burned as a sound technician? But this was crashing and burning in public. The cancellation was in newspapers all over the country. And oh, sure, I'd learned in my family that politicians lost elections and came back, but tanking in television news seemed so *permanent*. I was mortified. My ego was decimated. How could this have happened to ME? Wherever I went, I thought people were avoiding my glance. I had a dread disease: I'd been dumped! People treated me like I was contagious. They pitied me, for God's sake! What was I going to do now? My dream job gone. I was sure my career, if not my life, was over.

Looking back, I know that sounds overly dramatic, but that's what I felt at the time. I thought I was finished and was quite sure that everyone else thought so too. But I soon discovered I was wrong. In my failure, I started to hear from others who'd been through the same thing. They opened up and shared their stories. Walter Cronkite told me that when he was "retired" from the *CBS Evening News,* he thought his career was over, if you can imagine that now. Barbara Walters told me what happened when she coanchored the *ABC World News Tonight* and was canceled—which freed her up for the cosmic career she's had since. So many successful people told me they grew emotionally and were strengthened spiritually by falling somewhere along the road. It takes time, but it happens.

For me getting canned made me fearless about my career. It gave me the strength to follow my gut, to be myself on the job. In fact, I think I did some of my best work on the *Morning News* after we got canceled.

CBS News had given the show, the time period, the whole enchilada to the entertainment division. We had just one final month on the air. During that month I didn't care about anything the powers that be had to say about my work or what we were doing. I'd lost all respect for them, their opinions, and the way they did business. Finally I was free to be *me* on the air, and I felt great about it. If Forrest and I were both interested in an interview subject, then we did the interview together—a no-no on the show, but we didn't care. If an interview was going great, we let it run into overtime. We were more natural, and we ad-libbed much more. We heard from plenty of people who couldn't understand why the show was being nuked. Neither could we.

The last day of the *Morning News* was very emotional for all of us who'd come through the news wars together. Forrest gave me a bracelet inscribed "To My Sister in Arms." Management had offered me other jobs at CBS, but I wanted out. When we signed off, I walked out of the CBS Broadcast Center on 57th Street, and I've never been back.

I went home to Los Angeles defeated, demoralized, and depressed—taking a bath in a well of self-pity. But as I've said, I've learned that when you fail, it's important to grow from the experience. Use it. Don't let it define you or destroy you. Most of all, don't let it stop you. Pick your head up, dust off your ego, and do what you're most terrified to do: Get back on that horse and ride.

One month later I took a 70 percent pay cut for a job at NBC News. Back to being a reporter again. In a way, back to the beginning again—and this time without the safety of my producer/mentor around. I was determined to work my way up again in stature and pay, and basically I have. I may never achieve the prominence and visibility and hours of airtime the *Morning News* gave me, but I did get my paycheck back up there—and my self-respect.

But best of all, I'm a different person today because I experienced that failure. I've learned how to handle disappointment and rejection. I've learned to hold my head up high and soldier on. And today if someone suggests that I change my hair, alter my voice—or worse, cross an ethical line for a story—I tell them NO from a position of inner strength and certainty, because what can they do to me? Fire me or cancel my show? Been there, done that. And you know what? So have other people worth their salt.

Today I often ask interview subjects what they regard as their greatest success and their greatest failure. Their failure stories illuminate their character far more than the successes. Often these people reveal that their greatest failure was permitting their personal lives to crack or crumble on the way to the top. Their honesty and openness has helped me stay focused on my priorities, what I want in my life.

Lesson

Before I failed, my work was the focus of my life. It's where I put all my intensity, intelligence, and effort. Never again will I make that mistake. Experiencing how suddenly I could lose my job, how quickly I could be replaced, how easily the workplace went on without me, made me determined to quit identifying myself through my career. Today my work is a big and fulfilling part of my life, but it's not who I am. Who I am is far different from who I was before I failed, and I'd never trade the experience. Which doesn't mean it didn't hurt. And to hell with what the Washington Post *said about my hair.*

6

❧

Superwoman
Is Dead . . . and
Superman
May Be Taking
Viagra

NOT ALL OF THEM, OF COURSE. MY HUSBAND WANTS me to make very sure to tell you he is a superman, and there's no Viagra within a fifty-mile radius of our house. But seriously, I mean it when I say Superwoman is dead. That means you *can't* do it all. And even more important: YOU DO NOT *HAVE* TO DO IT ALL.

You CAN'T have an exciting, successful, powerful career and at the same time win the mother-of-the-year award and be wife and lover extraordinaire. No one can. If you see successful, glamorous women on magazine covers proclaiming they do it all, believe me, you're not getting the whole story.

Women have been beating themselves up with the Superwoman Delusion for more than twenty years, and I for one think it's been harmful. When I graduated from college, the propaganda said the brass ring was within everyone's reach. I had an absolute conviction that if I applied myself, I'd be like Barbara Walters at work (in my dreams) *and* Mother Earth at home (always there, always patient, always kind, and still make the bed) *plus* dress like a model all the time (no sweatsuits) *and* rock and roll with my man at night. And trust me, if Martha Stewart had been on the scene then, I would have expected exquisite things from myself in the kitchen as well.

But as my mother taught me, LIFE IS A MARATHON. It's an endurance event played out over time. Once I was freaking out to my mother about not being good enough in any area of my life. She said, "Maria, you can have and be all the things you want to be. Just do it over a lifetime. Don't try to do them all at once, because you can't. If you try to, everyone around you will suffer—mostly you." It took me a long time to even begin to internalize that wisdom.

Now, you may say, "What the hell is Maria talking about? She *does* have it all, and she does *do* it all." Well, that's not true. I don't do it all. My career isn't in the same league as Barbara Walters' or Diane Sawyers' or Oprah Winfrey's. And I see women at my children's school who put June Cleaver *and* Martha Stewart to shame, not to mention me. My kids tell me about friends' mothers who sew their Halloween costumes. I'm in awe of these women. I can't thread a needle. Other kids' moms whip up gourmet dinners every night. My specialty is microwave popcorn. Forget about knowing the new math before the kids do or being really active in the PTA. And to hear my husband tell it, he's not getting enough of anything at home.

There are so many areas where I can't claim competence, let alone mastery. But I've learned to do a few things really well in the time I have and to ask for help with the rest. The most important job is not to beat up on myself. It's a no-win situation if, no matter what I accomplish, I tell myself it's not good enough. I have to stop setting myself up to feel inadequate.

The first way is to stop comparing myself—yourself—to anyone else. Comparing how you *feel* on the inside (bad) to the way someone else *looks* on the outside (great) is a losing proposition. It's an impossible standard. We will always come up short. Women in particular know what I'm talking about: We often compare ourselves to others *in order to* make ourselves feel bad.

Here's Maria's Recipe for Feeling Bad about Myself: I carefully choose as a basis for comparison someone who has a stellar career. Then I ignore any other problems she has, any sacrifices she's chosen to make. Next I discount any of my own assets—the talents, gifts, and abilities God gave me. Finally, I ratchet up my expectations for myself to way, way past what I'm capable of. And voilà! I feel like dirt. It's a recipe for depression. Comparing yourself to others rarely is in the service of self-improvement. It's usually in the service of bludgeoning yourself into hopelessness. Overcoming this tendency has been a real struggle for me.

I know I've been talking a lot about humility, but here we are again. HUMILITY MEANS ACCEPTING YOURSELF—with every plus and minus, every defect and asset, exactly as you are today. It's stepping back and appreciating the whole picture: where you are today, what you've done, what you want to do. Humility means neither beating the hell out of yourself nor glorifying mediocrity. Today's picture isn't set in stone. It will change. That's self-acceptance.

My dad always drove that point home: "You are you, and you are unique." He says, "Anybody who gets to be with you, work with you, or share your life with you is goddamn lucky." I try to keep that thought with me as I travel down the road. You'll need to remind yourself frequently that you're a worthy human being, because there will be people in your path who'll make it their business to tear you down (and especially if you're a woman, you may want to do it to yourself). I keep a little saying on my mirror that I read every morning and evening. It says, "I am creative, I am powerful, and I can handle it." Obviously there are times when I feel confused or inadequate, or I wouldn't have slapped that up on the mirror. I also keep in my wallet a yellowed note my dad wrote me many years ago. It says that I am special, that I am wise, and that he loves me. No matter what I've failed to do on any given day, no matter how inadequate someone has made me feel, every time I read that note I feel great. Feeling strong about yourself is what you'll need, because life and your own reaction to it may knock you off balance. Find some message, some thought, some prayer that helps you get there, and use it to get your strength back, your self back.

So don't set yourself up for failure by trying to win an award in every area of your life. But do set high standards for yourself. Decide what a realistic "excellent" means to you in each area and go for it. I'm not talking about settling. I'm talking about setting obtainable goals that will keep you stretching and growing.

When I find myself in a rut, and the stench of staleness is already creeping in, I try to shake myself awake by reassessing. For instance, for the last several years I've felt inept about computers. My five-year-old thinks I'm allergic to CD-ROMs. (Actually, I am. When I see a CD-ROM, I break out in self-doubt.) I am an Internet idiot. Now, I'd been utterly comfortable for years feeling dumb about computers ("That's just who I am"). Because I can be so self-critical, feeling stupid about some things seems normal and natural, and I can just live with it. But in a fit of self-examination, I became totally conscious of the fact that I could actually change. What a genius.

I made a New Year's resolution to learn more about computers than merely how to run the word processor on my NBC-issued laptop. And I'm determined to go online—which is as scary to me as going naked into a tornado on a unicycle. Now, years ago I would have become totally monomaniacal and bulldogged my way through this one, too, applying myself to the computer eighteen hours a day until I got as good as possible as soon as possible. Today I'm more realistic about myself and the time I have. I'm not willing to sacrifice time with my kids or my work to this computer project—but I'm also not willing to use those obligations as an excuse to settle for mediocrity. So I'm setting my standard high and shooting for it, slowly and steadily. Where am I finding the spare time to become cyber-savvy? I'm no longer lying around feeling bad about myself because I'm lying around. You'd be surprised how much time that frees up.

The key is to stop concentrating on the negative and turn positive. I try not to strain for a goal that I can't possibly achieve. I reach forward, beyond myself, stretching for the limits of what I can achieve today. I must admit I've learned some of this from my husband, who doesn't get paralyzed or beat himself up when he can't do something. He just keeps at it. And he's always learning something. He finds it pleasurable and satisfying. He looks for an activity where he *cannot* and tries to turn it into *can,* slowly, steadily, without embarrassment. He is totally willing to look like an idiot at tennis and golf, in order to learn how to play. He has a ball doing it, laughing at himself. He just accepts that he'll never be as good as Pete Sampras or Tiger Woods even when they were twelve years old. While striving for mastery, he just wants to keep improving—and he accepts wherever he is on the learning curve today. That's true humility, though in a million years I never thought I'd use that word to describe him.

But I do use that word to describe my mother. I hope and

expect that when I'm her age, I will have experienced every-thing I wanted to do. I'll have had a fine career in broadcast journalism, and I'll be proud of it. I'll have helped raise our four miracles from God (and not been driven into the loony bin by them). I'll have been an awesome wife in every sense of the word, and my husband will have been lucky to have spent his life with me. (I feel the same way about him—at least today.) I'll have been a good sister, and I'll have honored, respected, and admired both my parents for who they are as individuals, as a couple, and most important, as parents. I'll be okay with the fact that I never reached as many people as Oprah Winfrey, never wrote like Emily Dickinson, never acted like Meryl Streep, and never baked like (Help! She's everywhere!) Martha Stewart.

Your life is like a mosaic, a puzzle. You have to figure out where the pieces go and put them together for yourself. I have a young friend who just knew she could write a novel but wasn't doing it. She beat the living daylights out of herself for not being a starving artist. But at the age of thirty she met a mentor who told her if writing doesn't pay the bills, then stay at the job that does and write your novel after work. And that's exactly what she's doing now—pursuing her passion and lov-ing her life. All we Superwomen can ask of ourselves is to be outstanding, to keep at it, and to make peace with wherever we wind up.

Lesson

PERFECTIONISM DOESN'T MAKE YOU PER-FECT. IT MAKES YOU FEEL INADEQUATE. You are not worthless because you can't do it all. You are human. You can't escape that reality, and you can't expect to. Self-acceptance is the goal. If Shakespeare were a Superwoman, she might have said, "To be or not to be— takes time and wisdom."

7

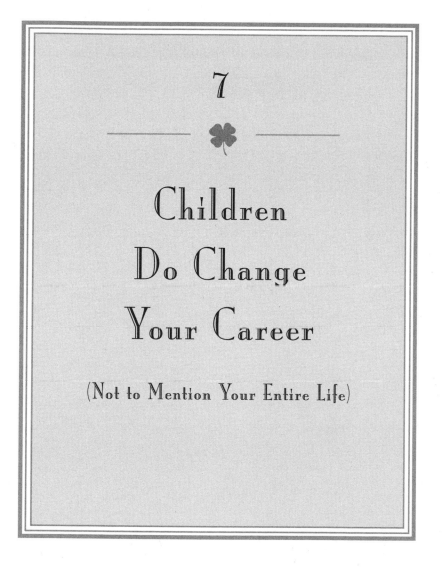

Children
Do Change
Your Career

(Not to Mention Your Entire Life)

THIS IS AN EXTENSION OF NUMBER SIX, WHICH SAYS, "You can't do it all." Once you have children, you not only can't do it all, you can't do it the same way you were doing it before. In other words, once you start a family, don't expect to be the same hard-driving, workaholic, do-anything, go-anywhere worker you were. Because if you are, your children will suffer— and believe me, if you think your children are suffering, the guilt will make your work suffer.

I waited a long time to start my family. I was thirty-four years old when our first daughter was born. And to tell you the truth, I was about as naive about childrearing as I was about the news biz that first day at the Philadelphia station. In fact, parenting has turned out to be a far bigger challenge than anything my journalism career has dealt me.

By the time our daughter was born, I was in love with my job. I was proud that after being fired/canceled/dumped from my highly visible post at the *CBS Morning News* three years before, I'd built myself back up at another network. I anchored two weekly NBC News broadcasts that I'd worked really hard to get and keep.

Everyone told me my schedule was nuts, but not to me. I was in heaven. I anchored both the weekend *Nightly News* out of New York and also *Sunday Today* out of Washington, D.C. Not so bad, you say? Well, I was living across the map in Los Angeles. I commuted from L.A. to New York on Friday, then to D.C. late Saturday night, and then back to the West Coast on Sunday. I loved the pace. I loved being out in the field doing stories, interviewing the likes of Cory Aquino, Fidel Castro, King Hussein. I loved traveling, and I loved anchoring. I loved the people I worked with, and I loved the challenge of the job and the stature I'd attained. This was what I'd worked so hard for all those years.

So when I got pregnant, I fully expected to keep visible on the air in both my anchor positions, because I couldn't imagine otherwise. Oh sure, I might have to slow down the pace a tad, but hadn't I been told I could/should be able to do it all? I expected nothing less from myself. (Which is why I thought it was perfectly natural to have a morning-sickness bucket next to the anchor chair. Or tear to the bathroom to throw up during a commercial and then race back to the anchor desk in time to smile and say, "Welcome back to *Sunday Today*.") I once even told a newspaper interviewer who asked about having a family on one

coast and a job on another, "I'm a firm believer, a religious person. . . . I believe that God is watching over this and that I'd be
able to do both." Writing that now, I can't believe how ignorant I
was. Or "arrogant" might be a better word—being quite sure that
what I wanted was what God wanted for me.

Reality started to set in the first time I held my daughter. I
fell deeply in love with my child and couldn't imagine being sep-
arated from her for one second. But even so, I held on to my
unrealistic expectations with both fists, spending most of my
maternity leave trying to figure out exactly how I was going to
manage this child and the travel and the job. I just knew I'd be
able to figure it out, but as I looked around me for guidance and
paths to follow, I found none. Apart from the impossible-to-get
morning news anchor jobs, which required hardly any travel,
there were few network news jobs that seemed compatible with
raising kids. And where were the role models? Many of the
women who'd risen through the ranks before me had to be single-
minded to get ahead in the male-dominated news business.
Many just plain stayed single. Many were divorced. Many had
no children. One big-time newswoman told me years later that
she still felt guilty she had sacrificed childrearing to career-
building.

And there was another pressure. My husband had made it
clear he had no desire to live in New York, where the NBC News
operation was based. His career was in L.A. and was much big-

ger than mine. So here I was with this beautiful baby and the man I loved in California, this job I loved in New York and Washington, and these stories I wanted to pursue were everywhere else.

So I went back to work and pretended nothing had changed, commuting like a maniac. My baby was accumulating frequent-flier miles. But it didn't take me long to realize I was kidding myself. Nothing was working—neither motherhood nor job. Whichever I was doing, I was worried and guilty about the other. Something had to give. I tried to convince my bosses to let me anchor at least one of the shows out of Los Angeles. "No way," they said. I went back home and cried in frustration. On top of everything, the very helpful advice people offered confused me even more. Some people suggested I just quit working and stay home and raise my child. I'm fortunate that was an option financially, but it just wasn't emotionally. Others suggested I keep my jobs, and everything would just magically work itself out, because I was such a good person and deserved to get what I wanted. That wasn't happening at *all*.

Finally I went to the head of the network with my dilemma. I told him I didn't think I could do the two anchoring jobs at the level I'd been doing them *and* raise my child *and* keep my marriage together. But, I told him, I didn't want to lose all I'd worked for either. He understood but also made it clear I had to choose. He told me that if I chose to give up my anchoring duties, other anchor opportunities would surely come along. Even though he was an honorable man, in TV news a promise like that is an empty one. But there I was at a crossroads. With a great deal of sadness, I gave up my East Coast broadcasts, both of them. And of course, the anchor chairs were filled in five minutes. The TV news machine just rolled on, and I went home to Los Angeles.

I'd like to tell you I felt relieved. The truth is, I felt like a failure again—so disappointed, because I'd been unable to figure out how to have it all. Sure I still was employed by the network doing one-hour specials, but I'd lost my power base, my own weekly shows. I was back to being a reporter, back to ground zero. Now, when I say ground zero, I know I'm being a drama queen. I know that really hitting bottom means being thrown out on the street with no job and no way to feed your kids. I know there are millions of women in truly dire situations who have only themselves to rely on. In fact, I seek out stories of women with children who have hit the bottom and pulled themselves up. I admire them, and I try to learn from their courage and strength.

Looking back now, I wish I hadn't wasted so much angst and so many tears on what in fact was my own choice. I was the one who chose to devote most of my time to my children and to work only part-time for NBC. And that's what I do to this day. I anchor and do pieces for a certain number of *Dateline* shows a year. My boss in New York works with me to find stories that don't involve too much travel, so I can tell myself it was worth my time away from my kids to do it. I anchor and report on at least two hour-long news specials of my own a year—for example, an hour broadcast about four women trying to get off welfare and into the job market in Wisconsin. And I have the great fortune to contribute to special coverage: conventions, elections, Olympics, inaugurations, and, yes, impeachment hearings. And with all that, I still have a great deal of freedom and flexibility and go to the studio only when I have to.

Keep in mind that when I made this arrangement with NBC more than a decade ago, I knew of no one else working part-time on a computer from home. And the head of the network did worry that if they opened that door for me, others would want to do it. But by then I'd worked my butt off in TV news for thirteen years—sometimes seven days a week, up to twenty hours a day. There was no place I wouldn't go for a story, no assignment I'd turn down. So when I said I'd like to set up stories and do as much work as I could from home, they knew I wasn't going to sneak off to the beach in Malibu and get a tan. It was clear I'd continue to work my butt off, but only part-time, while having babies and raising our family. And, they figured, if it didn't work out, they could always can me.

How lucky am I? *Very.* I had the financial ability to downsize my career, and I had employers who understood my priorities and were willing to work with me to maintain the strong and solid family life I wanted. Still, back when I made that choice, I felt so anxious and guilty. Had I known then that a decade later so many people would work out of their homes, I would have cried less and felt less lonely. Maybe not less guilty. To this day I get stabs of guilt that I have the opportunity to be fully involved in my kids' lives and still stay in a high-octane profession. I know that by working as long and hard as I did, I earned a certain amount of power and clout, and that helped me get my way. If I'd had my four kids back at the beginning in Philadelphia or Baltimore, forget it.

Let me say that I am more than grateful to the women who walked before me and broke down the barriers. There is no doubt in my mind that I wouldn't be able to work part-time and raise my children if the women before me hadn't worked their butts off to prove they could compete, that they were worth the corporate investment. We're worth having our needs accommodated.

Everyone's choices are different. You have to figure out what you need so you can look in the mirror and feel comfortable with the person you see. And you have to be honest about what you're willing to give up. My choice was to follow my gut and stay at home more. I know I'm unbelievably fortunate. If my gut had told me to work full-time, I could have well afforded the help that would let me do it. And today, I do know plenty of women who not only have kids, but also work much more than a forty-hour week. Their marriages are fine, their kids are flourishing, and so are their careers. I applaud them. It just isn't me.

There are all kinds of good mothers. Figure out what kind of parent you want to be—and don't compare yourself to anyone else. I had to have a conversation with myself. Which would make me feel worse: if my kids said, "You never help me with homework! You're never around!" or if Diane Sawyer got the Boris Yeltsin interview? For me, the first is worse, because I couldn't handle the guilt if my kids told me that. (Now I *am* around my kids all the time, and they say that kind of thing *anyway* to manipulate me. But the difference is, I let it roll off my back, because I know it's not true. If it were true, the guilt would be intolerable. And by the way, I don't presume to say I'd even win the Yeltsin interview, no matter how much time I did or didn't spend with my kids.)

Anyway, guilt is my gut talking to me, and I organize a lot of my life around guilt avoidance. There is a certain amount of attention and involvement I feel I need to give my children, and if it's less than that, I feel bad. Today my world revolves around their schedules, their traumas, their dramas. I have to be aware of what's going on in the classroom, what's happening with the homework, what the best friends are doing, and how all the little-girl and little-boy machinations and rivalries are playing out. My husband and I take the kids to school, pick them up, and shuttle them to soccer team and dance and play dates and doctor appointments. But I have the luxury of knowing if we can't do it, we have the childcare help we need.

Today overall, I spend much more time being a mother than trying to book an interview with the First Lady. The most important time on my clock is 3:30 P.M., when school is out. I try to turn the phones off from four to eight, so I can focus on playing with the kids and monitoring homework. Now, because of that, I've sometimes forgotten to follow up on interview calls. (Bye-bye, Yeltsin.) On the other hand, I did take my daughter to kindergarten one day in my sweats and full TV makeup and hair, and then changed clothes in the back of an NBC car on the way downtown for the O.J. Simpson verdict. So a normal mom I'm not.

And of course, since I *am* a driven overachiever, living with the choices I've made sometimes gives me a headache. Even after four children, I still get great assignments at work. But the fact is, I don't have my own show, and I don't have that power anymore. No, that high-pitched sound you hear is not whining. Well, maybe a little. I still get a stomachache when I lose a big-name interview to the anchorwomen who are on the air more, who have their own broadcasts and therefore greater stature. I'm out of that league now. And I do get my back up when people who see me with my kids day after day ask if I'm still working. But after my resentments subside and my ego chills out, I remind myself that *I'm* the one who took myself out of the big league. It was my own choice, and it was right for me. Still is.

To be sure, it's not always easy. I worry when I say no to a story that requires a lot of travel. Will this be the final straw for my bosses? Each time I turn down an assignment because it conflicts with a child's special performance or a soccer game, I hold my breath for their reaction. Will they fire me now? In my desire to be at home and hands-on, I have made some pretty reckless decisions.

Take the time I interviewed President Fidel Castro for a two-hour special on the Cuban Missile Crisis. It was a big deal, and NBC sent a huge team of producers and technicians to shoot it. We waited and waited. No Castro. Waited some more. No Castro. Now we were approaching the weekend. I was starting to sweat, because Monday was my daughter's first day in preschool. Her father was away on location, and I'd promised her nothing would keep me from taking her. In my mind, our first child's first day at school was as important as any world event. (First-time mother.) But as Friday came down in Havana, we were informed that Castro was sick—"under the weather," they said—and couldn't be interviewed yet. My boss said we'd wait for him.

Then on Saturday, Castro himself called me in for a meeting. I'd interviewed him before, and he wanted to tell me personally that he was still feeling sick and wouldn't be able to do the interview until Monday. My stomach tightened, and I blurted out, "I can't do that! I have to go back home to take my daughter to school!"

There was stone silence in the room. My boss kicked me under the table and asked me to step outside. "Are you nuts?" he asked. "Completely whacked out?" Didn't I know how long we had worked to get this interview? Didn't I realize if I left we would probably never get back in? Castro was so mercurial, you had to take him when you could get him. I understood all that, I told my boss, but I can't *not* go home. Looking back, my little girl probably would never have known what day the first day of school really was, but *I* knew. I went back inside and told Castro it was my first child and I just had to go, but I'd come back right after, if he would please wait. I thought my boss would have a seizure. But without skipping a beat, Castro said, "Take your daughter to school. I'll be ready next Saturday morning." And he walked out.

I flew home, took her to school (she didn't cry, but I did), and returned to Cuba to shoot one of the most fascinating interviews of my career. By the way, the first thing Castro said was, "How was the first day of school?" I dodged a bullet on that one.

And so my advice from the trenches is to work with your employers, if you can. Try to teach them about family-friendly policies, flexible hours, part-time work, and job sharing. If you want it but they don't get it, you might have to leave. There are too many businesses that value your family life now.

And remember, even though you may think your job is your life and your identity, it's not and it shouldn't be. At work, you're replaceable. Trust me, I know what I'm talking about. But as a parent you're irreplaceable. And by that, I mean mothers *and* fathers. Fathers also need to be reorganizing their lives for their children. Need I remind you it took two of you to make the child? My husband may not have altered his career to the extent I have since we've had children, but he has made changes, and he makes sure the people he works with understand his priorities. He brings our kids to work with him whenever he can, he plays sports with them, and he has a strong and loving hand in raising them.

But let me be clear. Neither of us thinks we two can raise our kids alone. I'd be dead without the participation and advice of my friends. Your friends help you, they spell you, they guide you, they cry with you when the pressure builds up. With their own children, they expand the cocoon of love and support that surrounds your family. What I said about looking for mentors in your work applies to childrearing as well. Never stop listening to good advice. Never be too smart to ask for help or so arrogant you think you can do it alone.

As a matter of fact, enlarging the circle of friendship to include all the Other Mothers is one of the blessings that came into my life after my career supposedly went south. I'd always expected I'd be operating professionally in what is still very much a man's world. But now I'm also a full-fledged member of the sisterhood of mothers—a gift that's enriched my life.

Lesson

Children do change your career. But they also open you up in ways you never imagined. Kids teach you things about yourself you couldn't learn on your own—lessons about patience and selflessness, love and letting go. In my life, I'd gone way past control freak all the way to control monster. But my children have taught me to let things roll off my back, to be flexible, to accept them even when they don't think/act/feel exactly as I do. I cannot control them, but I can guide and lead, honor and respect them. And believe me, they're much more fun than Boris Yeltsin.

8

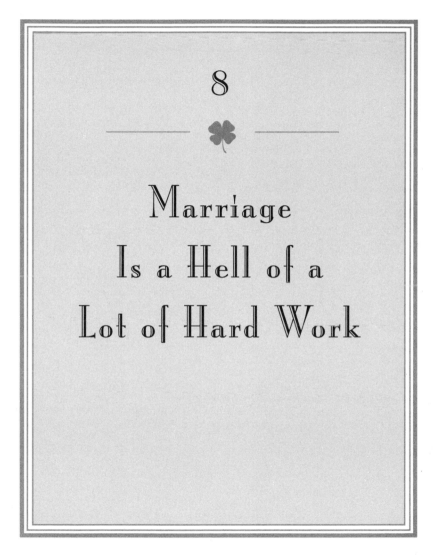

Marriage
Is a Hell of a
Lot of Hard Work

OH MY GOD, IS THAT TRUE. AND I HAD NO INKLING OF this when I left college. Otherwise I wouldn't have spent my twenties worrying that I wasn't married. In fact, if any of you is worried that you haven't run into anyone named Right, male or female, don't be in such a hurry. Chill, relax, and enjoy your freedom, because once you're married you don't have that kind of freedom anymore. After being in such a rush to meet their soul mates, so many people complain about being married to them. It's nuts.

Now, don't get me wrong. I'm happy in my marriage, and we've been in love for more than twenty years. I married a man who recognized I was an individual first and foremost and that my life apart from him was as important to me as our life together. I now know if I'd married someone who didn't want me to pursue my career, who didn't accept large Irish Catholic families, who wasn't crazy about kids, I'd be talking to you about *divorce* being a hell of a lot of work, instead of marriage. Which isn't to say my marriage has been easy.

When I graduated from college I dreamed not only of a fabulous career but also a storybook wedding. Let's call it the Wedding Delusion. Like many young women, I just assumed if I got the right man, the gorgeous dress, the drop-dead ring, and the extravagant wedding reception, poof! A one-way ticket to Happily Ever After. In short, I thought if I married the right person, I had it made. What an idiot. Making a commitment on your wedding day takes one little "I do." Living the commitment every day takes a lot of doing. In short, just because you know how to *get* married doesn't mean you know how to *be* married.

Comedian Jay Leno once said that anyone who says their marriage is hard work probably isn't in a very good marriage. Indeed, the word "work" sounds like drudgery and chores—like you wouldn't do it unless you got paid, and the pension benefits had better be good. But that kind of "work" isn't what I'm referring to in this chapter. No, my point is that marriage isn't just a state of being. It requires time, thought, and attention. It's a million separate actions taken in order to stay with someone, share a life with someone, have a partnership with someone, appreciate and support someone, cultivate love with someone—actions taken consistently over the long haul.

One thing that can kill a marriage right after the honeymoon is the Prince(ss) Charming Delusion. (Do I sense a theme here?) That's expecting your partner to do it all for you: make you happy, fix you, fulfill you, complete you, define you, make your life for you, make your life meaningful for you. Giant mistake. I was lucky and learned that before we got married. After a while together, my future husband said to me, "Don't expect or rely on me to make you happy." Well, I thought, isn't his grasp of the English language adorable. He doesn't realize what he's saying. Who else is supposed to make me happy, if not him? But he was adamant. "You must be happy with yourself first. Be happy with your life separate from what the other person brings to the table." This was serious. He told me he'd be the icing on the cake, but that I shouldn't expect him to be the whole dessert. Now, that definitely wouldn't make a good lyric for a romantic love song, but I knew he was right.

Love lessons from the trenches: WOMEN, don't expect a man to make your life and give you an identity. You must work at making your *own* life and identity. If you don't, I guarantee you'll have a distant, uninvolved, and resentful man on your hands— and you will be angry because he failed to fulfill your expectations. But your problem isn't your husband. It's your unrealistic expectations. And I say here to MEN as well (remember, I have four brothers), do not expect a woman to handle and arrange all the noncareer areas of your life *for* you, as if your job is *your* only responsibility in the marriage. You can't opt out of all the other areas of your own life. If you think that's just too much and you can't possibly help take care of business outside of your business, think again. Because if you don't, I guarantee you'll have a stressed-out, distant, and resentful woman on *your* hands—and *you* will be angry because she failed to fulfill your expectations. But your problem isn't your wife. It's your unrealistic expectations.

Men and women: There's no faster way to kill love than to blame the other party for not doing what you ought to do for yourself. To be sure, you can be blissfully happy with a partner, but you can't hold him or her responsible for making and keeping you happy. It's not fair, and it's not possible. If you set your partner up as your Higher Power, you'll wind up terribly disappointed and think it's *their* fault when they aren't. Give it up.

Moving right along to Happily Ever After. Guess what? Not. It's another delusion that creates crazy expectations. I have a really strong marriage, and I'm not a happy little wifey twenty-four hours a day. Things happen. My husband does things that tick me off, and God knows I do the same to him. There are stresses and pressures from outside that momentarily pull you apart or push you together. Even when nothing huge is happening, there are disagreements and arguments, times when you might even want to get the hell out. Life goes up and down, and so does the natural ebb and flow in a relationship. You're not *supposed* to be lovey-dovey all the time.

What happens if you don't deal with these negative situations and feelings that inevitably come up? Well, you can numb yourself with the Happily-Ever-After Delusion: "Everything's great! The kids are great! He's great! I'm great!" and shove any bad feelings underground. The only problem is it doesn't work. When you eventually concede that it's not all sweetness and light, you'll think there is something irreparably wrong with your marriage. And the truly sad part is you could have been dealing with each negative feeling and situation as you went along, so the little deals wouldn't fester into a great big deal.

Now, maybe you have no illusions about marriage. Maybe your parents divorced when you were a kid, so you already know that Happily Ever After exists only in fairy tales and movies. But many friends of mine who are children of divorce tell me that they, too, held on to the dream that they'd do it differently from their parents. They still wanted and expected a fairy tale.

In my case, my parents just made the whole thing look easy. If they fought, and I know they did, they just did it away from us. If they had different opinions about childrearing, they worked it out in private, and we never knew about it. Smoothly and seamlessly they alternated between doing their own thing as individuals and operating as a couple, and we all functioned together as a family. But since they never talked about the work a marriage required, I expected that my own married life would unfold the same way—naturally, nicely, smoothly, happily.

So here's my advice: If you get along with your parents and

respect their opinion, ask them about the good and bad in their marriage. Ask them how kids affected their relationship. Ask them how they've handled money and whether that affected the power balance between them, because it can. Ask them about religion, ask them about everything. Pick their brains and get their wisdom. If your parents are like mine, they'll prefer not talking about any rough spots in their road. They'll try to gloss over any difficulties they might have had—perhaps out of fear you'll think less of them. Tell them you need them to be honest and open and that you won't judge them, that you want to learn the things they wish *they* had known, things they might have done differently, the lessons they've learned. If your parents' marriage didn't survive, ask them why. If they made mistakes, you can learn from them.

When I meet a couple today that's been married for a long time, I ask them how they do it. (My husband says I'm always conducting interviews.) No matter who they are, they have something to teach me. One thing I hear over and over from couples who've made it work is that you must have respect for your partner, and you must be able to practice the art of forgiveness. A great girlfriend of mine is blissfully, happily married. I asked her how she does it. She told me that she and her husband practice what she calls *automatic forgiveness*. "If one of us hurts the other's feelings or does something to infuriate the other—and that happens very often, because we're sensitive to each other—then you have to get mad, let it be known, have a little or big fight about it, and then let it go and move on." That's forgiveness—not holding on to and cultivating the feeling that you've been wronged and then parading around like a wounded martyr.

Forgiveness is not having to stay *right*. You can actually *be* right, let it be known, and then stop bludgeoning your partner with it. Let it go and move on. My friend says, "I keep trying to remind myself that I love this man and to get past the anger and return to the love as soon as I can. Go with the love," she says. "This is how to stay married and not stay miserable." Smart, wise advice you can use, and it works. Practice being good at forgiveness before you say "I do."

Also make sure that you have a great time on your own before you get married. You'll have a great time after you get married, but it's just a different kind of great time, if you catch my drift. Enjoy your freedom. Spend as much time as you can getting to know yourself and what you want and need. And then keep your eyes open for that great love to appear—that person who loves you for you.

And by the way, make sure you love that person for him/herself, too. Chances are remote (i.e., one in a zillion) that you'll get your partner to change. They won't. Certainly, the things you find most annoying and objectionable won't ever change. What does change over time is your own willingness to accept these things. And make sure you tell your partner your personal dreams for yourself and for both of you as a couple. Make sure you are on the same wavelength about kids, money, religion, and the way you want to live.

But, please, don't expect your prospective mate to be the be-all and end-all—to have *all* the same interests, to want to talk about *all* the same things. No one person can do it all for you. Didn't you ever notice that's why you have a variety of friends? Friends are people who reflect different aspects and interests of your life. For me, there are the other mothers, the work partners, the diet buddies, the gossip hounds, the soul sisters. It's a hand-picked support network tailor-made by me for me—especially important since I have no biological sisters. They help me with the kids, tell me I don't have to be Superwoman, warn me if I'm not being true to myself, and scream that I don't have to lose an-other five pounds. Girlfriends are the ones who fill in the gaps and pick up the slack left by your primary relationship. That's what friends are for.

My own life has taught me that even if you do all of this work before you get married, you'll need some luck, and you'll have to be willing to give 100 percent. Even then your marriage might not work. If it doesn't, please don't beat yourself up about it for the rest of your life. Get help quickly so you can handle it well. A girlfriend at work did just that. She and her husband really and truly put their child's best interest first. They got help and now are great friends who share parenting, their joys, their sadness. They just don't share their bed.

Looking back at my own life, I thank God I didn't get married until I was thirty. I met my future husband when I was twenty-one—two months after I got out of school, in fact. I fell in love with him immediately. (More about that later on.) But I still wasn't sure what I was doing and where I was going in my life. I was still scared and insecure, not yet strong enough to handle what this guy would throw my way.

As I worked my way up in my career, I learned more about myself, and I gained self-confidence. And as I was getting to know myself, so was he. Over several years, he actually observed what's important to me. He saw that, like him, I'm extremely ambitious, that my family is everything to me, that religion is a big part of my life. He learned that I like to talk, that I'm curious, athletic, hot-tempered, and used to getting my own way. In other words, he realized that I would be a handful as a wife. (And I would have had to have been deaf, blind, and incredibly stupid not to see that he was more than a handful himself.)

He decided to marry me anyway. Lucky for me, my husband hasn't asked me to change. Sure, he's dropped hints that I should slow down, that I talk too much and ask too many questions, and that I'm a control freak. But he's never asked me to stop being me. And I return the favor.

I practice the art of forgiveness, and so does he. We have to.

There's a great deal my husband and I don't agree on. Don't even get me started on that. And no doubt it would have been easier if I had married the boy next door or even a boy from the United States. But I didn't. I fell in love with a boy from Austria who couldn't have been more different from what I imagined for myself, but I went with the love. I went with my gut—and so far, so good.

Lesson

Across the years that I've worked in newsrooms, so many of my coworkers have been divorced—and to tell you the truth, that has scared me. An all-consuming career often doesn't leave room for a spouse. Today I spend a lot of time on my marriage. I pay attention to it. I make it a priority to connect with my husband and nurture the relationship. Please focus on your marriage. Don't take it for granted. Choose to spend time together when you can, even on days you don't want to. Our lives are so busy, we can't let too many opportunities to be together slip by. That's the "work" part—working it in.

9

※

Don't Expect
Anyone Else
to Support You
Financially

MAYBE YOU'RE LUCKY ENOUGH THAT YOUR PARENTS are rich. Maybe you'll marry into money. But please don't rely on it. Work for your money. Make your own way. Live within your means. There's nothing better for building genuine self-worth and self-respect.

You might be wondering what this has to do with me—or with you. You may be sitting on loans up the wazoo. You may be working full-time and going to school full-time, or juggling multiple jobs to make ends meet. If that's the case, I take my hat off to you. You can probably skip this chapter. But it's not that long, so it won't kill you to read it.

I'm one of the lucky ones whose parents paid for their college education. I got out of school knowing I wanted to work, knowing I had to work, but also knowing, at least somewhere in the back of my head, that I wasn't going to starve if I didn't get a job. Now it just so happens that my passion can pay well, and I've stayed in it long enough to get one of those jobs with a big salary. And I'm doubly fortunate. Knowing my parents, I think if my passion didn't pay the bills, they would have helped me. But looking back, I'm really glad I never asked them. Instead I learned something important: that I could take care of myself.

When I started working, people assumed I didn't have to work for the money. They thought since I was from a wealthy family, the whole work thing was just a lark. (Remember that news director in Philadelphia.) Then when I got married, I can't tell you how many people thought I'd quit my job—even told me to do so—because now I'd captured a man who could support me. I can't describe how mad that made me. I remember running into a well-known agent about six months after I got married, when I'd started my new job at NBC after the *CBS Morning News* went down the tubes. He kissed me hello, asked me about the new network, then shook his head and said, "I don't know why you bother with all that network news crap. You married a rich guy. Sit back, enjoy, have a few babies and a nice life." I wanted to punch the guy's lights out. I'm glad I didn't, because he wasn't the last one to say that, and you can't punch everybody's lights out.

I did not get married to live off my husband. I did not go into the television news business for the money. In fact, when I went into the business, the pay was nothing like it is today. I work because I love it, and I love earning my own money. It makes me feel strong and independent to know I can make my own way financially. If you want to feel emotionally independent, knowing you can earn your own money is key.

My regret in this area is that I never took the time to be really smart about finances. Advice from the trenches: Don't do what I did. I never paid attention to what I was doing with what I was earning. When I graduated, most of the women in my class didn't talk about money. We had it or we didn't have it. Either way, we didn't even think about it. I was never great in math so I just assumed some guy would take care of it for me, or that it would magically take care of itself. Big mistake. This is definitely something I would change about my life. I would make sure that from the outset I spent as much time learning how to handle my finances as I did climbing up the career ladder.

In this day and age it's really stupid to be stupid about financial matters. It doesn't do you any good to make the money if you don't know what to do with it other than spend it. A girlfriend of mine who has earned more money than God shared some great advice she got at the beginning of her career from a well-known old entertainer. He said that no matter how wealthy she got, she should go over all her cancelled checks with an eagle eye. He said it would make her smart about money, make her aware of where her money was going, and what she wanted it to do for her.

Now that I'm earning good money, how to handle it has become a real challenge for me. I'm trying to get smart about money management, estate planning, you name it. I'm playing catch-up in a world that is changing and moving so rapidly, it's hard not to feel like I'm always behind the curve. I don't think I'll ever have fluency in this area, and it really ticks me off.

So, please be smarter than I was—especially you women. Don't just assume that a man will take care of this for you. If you take time off from your career or leave it entirely to take care of your children—the hardest work for no pay, but don't get me started—please don't check out of this arena. You never know if you'll be blindsided by life and thrown into a situation where you will have to know how to take care of yourself. And believe me, learning about this stuff takes time, and the people who can teach us aren't always so patient with those of us who are idiots about it. Advice from the trenches: Learn about money and talk openly about it in your relationship.

Now, I do very well in the salary department, but as you know, my husband does a lot better. He says he doesn't have more power in our marriage because of it, but I think he does. I don't want to ask him for money, and I don't. It probably sounds crazy, but that's just my pet peeve. He's incredibly generous and always says it's "our money," but I just like knowing that I can bring home the bacon too. I just wish I were as smart about business as he is.

Another thing about making your own money: There may come a time in the not-too-distant future when you'll want to—

or have to—help your parents financially. If you're smart about your money now and bust your butt and get lucky, you might be fortunate enough to be able to help out.

One final note. You may not think it right now, but I bet you won't need all the money you'll earn. I bet there'll be times when you can give some part of your income to charity. I admire the well-known sports agent who will not sign players unless they agree to give 10 percent of their income to charity. I also admire a young woman who helps me with my kids. She's Mormon and has always given 10 percent of her earnings to her church—never thinks about it, just plans for it and does it. I greatly respect her and so many other young people I've met who start with that kind of good heart right out of the gate. I believe it comes back to you tenfold in spiritual gifts—like gratitude, self-worth, and peace of mind.

Lesson

Money gives you options, but only if you don't fritter it away. Pay attention to where your money is going, so it can help you get where you're going. And remember: You may never be able to have it all—but it's good for the soul to give away some of what you do have.

10

Laughter

GOTTA HAVE LAUGHTER. IT'S THE LAST ITEM ON THE list, but it's the one that makes the first nine doable. Life isn't smooth, but you can survive the kinks and curves by laughing at them—and yourself.

People always ask me what attracted me to my husband. It was his sense of humor. Take my advice. Pick your partner not only for the lust, but for the laughter. Trust me. You'll need humor much more than you'll need money, a great job, a fabulous wardrobe, or even being thin.

The first day I met my husband, he said something totally irreverent and funny to my mother. Most people are terrified of my mother. But when he was introduced to her, he said, "Your daughter has such a great ass!" I don't know how he gets away with that kind of thing, but my mother laughed her head off.

This was at a pro/celebrity tennis tournament more than two decades ago. He wasn't a celebrity yet, but he was something of a cult figure. My brother suggested it would be cool to have this amazing professional bodybuilder play against the pros. He had a blast. He poked fun at himself—his thick accent, his middle European wardrobe, his lack of tennis talent. I laughed so hard I fell in love.

Everyone I knew was quite sure I was just being rebellious, infatuated with how different he was. All I knew was that every time we got together, we had so much fun. He was smart, ambitious, eager to learn, and he helped me to take myself, my heritage, and my "destiny" far less seriously. By now, we've been together for twenty-two years. Of course it hasn't always been fun, because life isn't only fun, but I can honestly say no one else can make me laugh more than he does. No one else I know looks at life quite the way he does. Today whenever our lives feel pressured, whenever he gets to raging about whatever reversal or frustration—and he does that a lot—I say, "Where's your sense of humor? I can't believe you're not making me laugh about this." He usually takes the cue and bounces back.

I don't know anyone who has more fun than my husband. He works like a dog, but he's got a wonderful ability to turn it off and go play. He surrounds himself with people who make him laugh (mostly guys who get nuts with those stupid macho jokes I don't get), and he immerses himself in hobbies that he enjoys. As a matter of fact, *I* get great joy teasing him about his hobbies—riding motorcycles with the boys, shooting pool with the boys, smoking cigars with the boys, skiing and hiking with the boys, and most recently, playing the dreaded golf with the boys. I tell him that all these things take him away from me, that he's just being selfish. (As if it were desirable to be miserable together.) I needle him that the only reason he gets to enjoy himself is because I hold down the fort with the kids.

The truth is, I give my husband grief because I'm jealous he's figured out a way to live his life so that he still has loads of laughs. He's just done a better job managing his time and being able to say no to things he doesn't want to do. (This one is a big issue for most women.) The truth is I know many more men than women who are able to steal time away for themselves.

Well, that's the female propaganda anyway. Here's the truth about women: We have our own secret hobby, and that's stealing away time to gab. This is one of our greatest pleasures, and we never deny it to ourselves. Girlfriends make each other laugh. We laugh about out own situations and frustrations. We laugh about our kids. But mainly, we laugh about our guys—like the way they stroll around those big green fields telling dirty jokes and chasing after little white balls.

Laughter infuses your life with joy. Believe me when I tell you I know so many people my age—not *that* old—who've lost the joy in their lives. And I'm not even talking about the tragedies and troubles that befall all of us. Life's awesome responsibilities have a way of creeping up on you, wearing you down, making you dead serious, robbing you of laughter and joy.

I hear it from people my age all the time. They say, "I'm not having any fun anymore. I can't remember the last time I laughed till I cried. I can't remember the last time I felt free." They let the joy go.

Remember back in the first chapter, where I talked about "pinpointing your passion"? I told you one of the things that fed my passion for the news was how much fun the boys in the back of the campaign plane were having. I hope there are people in your workplace who make you laugh. I hope you can see the humor in your changing situation as you scoot up that ladder.

You remember my first producer at CBS News, my mentor? Well, I told you how nuts she was, but I probably didn't do her sense of humor justice. Or her laugh. She has one of the most outrageous, loudest laughs I've ever heard. The more insane the situation, the funnier she makes it. And we laughed so much working together that that old cameraman—the one who blistered my hide for making that little speech in the trailer park—used to call us Fluffy and Flako. We never could figure out which of us was which, and we laughed about that too.

We had a lot to laugh about. Just one story: finding ourselves in a huge crush of cameras and reporters—in our business, we call it a "gang-bang," I'm sorry to say—at the Cannes Film Festival. The European press corps was chasing after Robert DeNiro, who had no intention of being interviewed. My producer was mortified to be caught up in the crush—"for an entertainment story, for God's sake." After all, she was training me to be a Hard News Hannah, and this was years before O.J. and Di and Monica. But we got swept up in the competition of it, pushing and shoving, and I actually found myself crawling on all fours under a table and popping up right next to DeNiro. My producer shoved our cameraman across the table into DeNiro's face and asked him the stupidest thing I'd ever heard come out of her mouth: "So. Do you like your movie?" We both broke up. (DeNiro didn't.) We felt so bad about ourselves, we washed it away in rivers of laughter. You have to laugh at yourself if you do something stupid or jerky—especially if that's the only way you're going to get a laugh that day at all.

I've laughed my way through all my ups and downs in TV news. In fact, I've laughed on the air when I shouldn't have. The first time I anchored the *CBS Morning News,* sort of an audition, I was so nervous that I spent the previous minutes before the show dry-heaving in the bathroom. (What *is* it with my stomach?) I had no idea how to anchor, and true to the news biz, nobody told me how, either. I was supposed to do the top of the show. The lead stories were strung together on videotape, and I was to read the headlines that went with the pictures. But I was so nervous, I raced through the headlines like a maniac, paying no attention to what pictures were showing when. I finished talking way too early—and as I saw the pictures continuing to play silently on the monitor, proceeded to laugh my head off. On the air. (I guess that didn't bother anyone, because I got the job. Which tells you something.)

One morning I was to interview our top Middle East correspondent about some burning situation in that part of the world. During the commercial before our segment I told him that when we were done he should get out of the way, because we'd be going straight to another segment. And he did. We finished our interview, and as I turned to the second camera for the next intro, I could see our distinguished veteran war correspondent out of the corner of my eye, crawling on his hands and knees under the cameras to get off the set. I broke out into peals of laughter and couldn't stop.

I have so many memories that make me laugh. Back to Cuba. The first time I was there, I remember standing next to Castro while he screamed bloody murder at me in rapid-fire Spanish, because the week before, the *NBC Nightly News* had done a story about a Cuban landing strip being used for drug trafficking. It was all I could do not to bust out laughing. Here was a head of state in fatigues with high-heeled combat boots standing in a beaten-down shack in Havana, screaming to *me* in a language I didn't understand about editorial policy I didn't make a thousand miles away in Rockefeller Center. I don't know if I wanted to laugh because it seemed funny or to relieve the tension. In fact, I did laugh. If you ever find yourself in a similar situation, I don't recommend it.

I've been blessed to have been able to work with so many funny people. They may not always know they're being funny, but by and large the people in my profession have a great sense of humor. Trust me, when you're racing against demon deadlines, doing live shots from crime scenes or conventions or courtrooms, facing crushing competition, always trying to do the impossible in an impossible time frame, you need people around you who can laugh. Because otherwise everything gets so life-and-death serious, it can make you sick.

I've asked myself where I learned to be both so ambitious and driven on the one hand, and so willing to laugh at myself on the other. I think I've figured it out. My mother.

My mother made it very clear to me that it was a man's world, and it was no use complaining about it. From the time I was little, she pushed me to do whatever my brothers did. "Just get in there, Maria. Get in there and do it." If it was a boys-only football game, she made sure I played, no matter how disgusted they were at the prospect. But really it was up to me to participate. "Get in there, Maria. Get in there and play," she pushed me. And I'd shove my way in. For a long time my brothers wouldn't throw the football to me. They barely talked to me in the huddle. They just told me each time that I'd be the hiker, the one who passed the ball between my legs to a brother, who'd then get to put it into play. They liked that, because they made fun of my butt sticking up in the air. The play swirled all around me, but no matter; my mother said I was really in the game and that was what was important. After what seemed like several years of football games, they finally threw the ball to me and tackled me. At last! It wasn't all that different from when they'd pile on and tickle me to distraction, but I was playing football! I was so bad at the game compared to them, I had to laugh at myself. They certainly did. And I grew up with that voice in my ear—"Get in there, Maria. Just get in there and do it!"—and also the sound of laughter, me laughing at my own nerve. The lesson I learned was to take what I *do* seriously, but not take *myself* so seriously.

Sometime when you have a free moment, write down what has given you joy in your life. What have you been happiest doing? What's been fun? What has made you laugh till you cried? Keep that paper and look at it every couple of years. You'll be surprised how quickly you forget to do those things, so caught up are you in getting ahead and taking yourself too seriously. When you feel a lack of laughs in your life, look at your list and do one of the things on it. Put some of the joy back in.

I did something like that last year. I felt I was missing the fun I'd experienced in my twenties and figured I needed an attitude adjustment. So I sat down and asked myself what I did back then that made me so happy. What made me laugh? To be honest, some of the things I couldn't do again, and I won't get into what those were. But I remembered what a great time I used to have playing sports. So I've started playing tennis and biking with my kids. And I remembered how much I laughed when I spent time with my brothers and my cousins. So I've made a point to schedule family vacation time every summer with them back East where I grew up. That week of laughter feeds my soul all year long. And instead of blowing off my high school reunion, I went to it and laughed at memories with old girlfriends. And I've been reminding myself about having more humility. I find when I have an accurate picture of myself—and accept and appreciate where I am in my life and where I still want to go— that's when I have the perspective and attitude that allows me to enjoy myself and have a good laugh.

Lesson

When I was a girl, if you'd have told me I'd be married to an Austrian-born, Republican bodybuilder whose big breakthrough was playing Conan the Barbarian, I would have laughed out loud. But that's what happened, and I'm still laughing. The love and the laughter are what you need most in your life. They'll fill out all the potholes in the road.

And that's my top ten list of things I wish I'd known—my report from the fighting front, as a college graduate making it day by day out there in the Real World.

I wish I could tell each and every one of you that you'll achieve greatness in whatever you do. Let me be the first to tell you—you may not. But you can achieve happiness and a rich life by taking your time, keeping it simple, and getting down on your knees every once in a while to thank God for what you have and to ask Him for the faith, love, guidance, and humility we all need to get through this life.

As you step out of college into the rest of your lives, I know you're wondering whether that jittery feeling in your gut is excitement or just plain fear of the future. Believe me, it's fear. Fear of the unknown and fear of failure—in love and in life. It's all right and perfectly normal and natural to be anxious about what's around the corner. But never let that stop you from looking around the corner to see what's there for you.

Each and every one of you is an awesome, powerful, resilient human being capable of living the life you design for yourself. It's within you to carve out your own future, create your own destiny. You're in a glorious moment, filled with possibility. Try to keep this feeling of endless possibility alive as long as possible. Whenever you feel it fading, call it back and renew it. That's a gift you can give yourself. You deserve to feel great about your life.

Someone wise once told me that courage is walking through your fear with faith. I wish all of you the faith and the courage to pinpoint your passion. Now go out there, be free, and achieve it. Congratulations!

Afterword

I gave that speech and wrote this book so that you might be spared. Not from having to learn the lessons I had to learn. No one can spare you that, because learning is experiential, and you have to do it yourself. As a wise person once told me, and it actually was the same wise person as before: "If I could spare you the pain you're experiencing, I wouldn't—because I wouldn't want to deprive you of the strength and wisdom you'll gain from having gone through it and come out the other side."

So what I wish to spare you is the loneliness and shame I had. I thought I was the only one who kept starting at the bottom. I thought I was the only one who was scared. I thought I was the only one who'd ever failed. I thought I was the only one who couldn't be Superwoman. Now I hope you know that these things happen. They're *normal*. When you experience failure or rejection or disappointment, you'll be able to tell yourself, "I haven't crashed into a brick wall. I've only hit a speed bump."

You can survive and move on. I did, and that's the message of hope I pass along to you: If I can do it, you can do it too.

Everybody's tragedies are their own. If you're smart and keep your eyes and ears open, you'll hear the stories of people who've survived the unimaginable—who've persevered and endured, despite the loss of loved ones, despite sickness, divorce, bankruptcy, addiction, you name it. "If they can do it, I can do it too."

You know, after I gave that speech, I came up with a list of other Things I Wish I'd Known:

> I wish I'd known that in the scheme of things, a big, expensive wedding is a silly waste of time and money and angst.

> I wish I'd known how easy it is to lose touch with your college friends. Before you know it, twenty years have gone by, and you let your pals slip away. Try not to let that happen to you.

> I wish I'd known that computers were going to rule the world. I would have tried for mastery sooner.

> I wish I'd known how creative, crucial, and consistent sex would have to be. And I certainly never knew I'd wind up talking about it so much.

> I wish I'd known how quickly careers take over your life. I dove into mine right after college. I wish I'd taken a

year off just to play around—a year with no responsibilities, no deadlines, no goals. Once you're trying to make it, you can't be carefree like that again.

➤ I wish I'd known how important my health would be. I'd have taken better care of myself earlier. Now that we know we can learn and grow and change in our forties and fifties and way beyond, it's a crime to let our bodies deteriorate from neglect or misuse.

➤ I wish I'd learned earlier about "the simplicity movement"—very wise people who are simplifying their lives by finding quiet corners where they can contemplate what's really important and then shed the excess. (Maybe I couldn't really do that until I'd cluttered up my life so much, it required cleaning out.)

➤ I wish I'd known earlier how to say NO. What I'm realizing is that really smart people don't burden themselves with guilt. They're comfortable saying, "No, I can't do one more thing." They just manage their time very well. They do *not* do it all, but whatever they do, they do well. This is my goal today.

➤ I wish I'd known how transforming is the love a parent feels for a child. I would have been a different child to my parents—kinder, more open, sharing more with them. In my self-seeking, I turned away from them too quickly and easily. Now I've learned that kids can hurt your feelings very deeply. (The other day my younger daughter said, "Mommy, you're gonna have to get your own play dates, because we've been playing with you too much. We want to play with our own friends more!" That cut me to the quick.)

➤ I wish I'd known, too, how difficult it was for my parents to watch me marry and move three thousand miles away. I'm already preparing myself to be as gracious, loving, and generous when one of my own kids does something like that to me down the road.

➤ I wish I'd known my parents when they were young. I met these two extraordinary individuals when they were halfway through their lives. I wish I'd been able to experience them before they were saddled with us kids.

➤ I wish I'd known my four brothers would end up being my best friends. I would have hit them less when we were kids, thrown them out of my room less, and dismissed and discounted them less. Today they're *not* just wallpaper, they are a crucial part of my life—always there. I don't take their love for granted. We've worked deliberately and hard to create our own separate relationships apart from our parents—and that's become more crucial as we've aged. As a matter of fact, we make it a point a couple of times a year to get together, just the five of us in a room, to find out where each of us is and how we're *really* doing, to clear up any resentments or misunderstandings, to just *be* there for each other. My family relationships, nurtured in my adulthood, are the backbone of my life, the skeleton that the rest of it hangs on.

➤ I wish I'd known earlier in my life the importance of saying "I love you." You'd be surprised how many people don't really know how much they're loved. I've learned to say it—to my kids, my husband, my parents, my brothers—whenever I get that feeling in my heart. I also tell my friends that I love them, that they're important to me and I'm grateful for their friendship. You know, I've learned a terrible truth from going to too many funerals in my life: So much of the praise comes after people are gone, in their eulogies. We ought to be telling them sooner. So I'm a big believer in toasting people at birthdays and anniversaries, family gatherings, special celebrations—toasting their great qualities, their friendship, their wisdom, their uniqueness. What could be better than being told out loud in a genuine way, with other people listening, that you are loved, respected, needed, appreciated, and adored?

➤ I wish I'd known that God would give me all the strength and faith I needed to go through some of my own tough times—my husband's open-heart surgery, the death of close relatives, the illness of children. Perhaps I wouldn't have been so afraid.

➤ I wish I'd known how often I'd reinvent myself. Here I had focused all my energy and juice on becoming the best newswoman I could possibly be, and boom! At the age of forty-three my interests changed dramatically. I woke up one day and wrote a children's book. Suddenly I was an author—a new identity for me, and I was starting over again. It reinvigorated me, got me excited again, passionate again. And here I am now, writing yet another book. I really wish I'd known there isn't just one answer to the question "What do you want to be when you grow up?" Because it turns out I grew up to be a hard-driving career woman in my twenties, a wife and mother in my thirties, and all that plus an author in my forties. I'm grateful I've gotten in touch with the part of us that's teachable and renewable, fresh and growing. We *can* reinvent ourselves and find a whole new world out there—or a whole new world within ourselves. Over and over again.

➤ I wish I'd known how to be at peace with myself sooner. I don't think I was ever truly proud of myself until one day in April 1999, when I learned both that I'd won a Peabody Award for Broadcast Journalism and that my children's book had made the *New York Times* best-seller list. I sat in my hotel room and wept. After forty-three years on this planet, I felt I'd accomplished something. I was being recognized not for my family or my husband or my looks, but for myself and my own hard work. It told me I had a right to be proud of myself. Finally.

Okay. Now I'm totally sick of talking about myself. Go take what I've learned and run with it. I'll get back to you in a decade or so and give you an update. God bless you and good luck!